STANLEY TUCCI

Biography

FLAVORS OF MY JOURNEY

Table of Contents

Chapter 1. A CHILDHOOD IN KATONAH

Chapter 2. RETURN TO THE U.S.

Chapter 3. TWO DOLLARS, ONE DREAM, AND A PASTRAMI SANDWICH

Chapter 4. SALT, BUTTER, AND THE SHAPE OF MEMORY

Chapter 5. MERRY CHRISTMAS! (AND OTHER WARNINGS)

Chapter 6. SECONDO'S SILENCE

Chapter 7. THE ANDOUILLETTE OFFENSIVE

Chapter 8. THE WEDDING FEAST

Chapter 9. COMMUNITY TIES

Chapter 10. COOKING, CLEANING, CRYING

Chapter 11. COOKING IN THE DARK

Chapter 12. THE END

Chapter 13. COOKING RECIPES

Chapter 1.

A CHILDHOOD IN KATONAH

I grew up in Katonah, New York, a beautiful community about 60 miles north of Manhattan. We moved there when I was three years old from Peekskill, New York, a little town on the Hudson River with a large Italian population where my father's family had settled after arriving from Calabria. Northern Westchester's suburbs were not nearly as densely populated in the 1960s and 1970s as they are today, making them ideal places to grow up. My sisters and I had a fantastic group of friends who lived on or near our neighborhood and with whom we played almost every day, mostly outside. There were no video games or cellphones, and television was only occasionally seen. Instead, we spent the entire year playing in each other's yards or neighboring fields, primarily in the woods. The woods had everything we needed. Endless trees to climb and create "forts" in, frozen marshes to walk through or skate on, stone walls from the Revolutionary War to climb, and slopes to sled down when covered in the deep snow that used to fall every winter. Now that I am in my sixties, I constantly wish I could return to those times, that place, and my innocent, engaged, enthusiastic self. I'd like to go back just to have my beautiful head of hair back. The unfettered activities outside in all types of weather were a wonderful part of my childhood, but what and how my family cooked and ate was far superior. Food preparation, serving, and consumption were the key activities and topics of discussion in my early home. My mother maintains that when she married my father, she could only heat water. If this is right, she has more than made up for it over the last 50 years. I can honestly say that my mother never made a bad dinner on the four-burner electric stove she used throughout my youth, nor on the gas hob that replaced it many years later. Not even once.

Every day, like many suburban children growing up in 1960s America, I would bring lunch to school. It was unusual for me to buy a meal at the cafeteria. This was due to two things. For one thing, it was excessively expensive for my parents to do so, and the food served in the cafeteria was terrible. Anyone growing up in America at the time understands what I'm saying, so I won't go into detail. Despite the fact that many of my peers carried their lunches, the contents of my lunchbox differed significantly from those of my classmates. My portable childhood dinner, painstakingly packed into a pop-image-themed metal container (often known as a Partridge Family or Batman lunch box), would look like this: Sandwich scrambled egg, fried potato, and sautéed sweet green pepper between two slices of Italian bread, or in a "wedge" or "hero," which is a huge loaf of Italian bread sliced horizontally and filled with whatever you like. In Philadelphia, they're known as "hoagies."

Only one slice of fruit. (A pear, apple, or orange.)

One store-bought, highly processed, premade dessert. Twinkie, Devil Dog, Ring-Ding, or Ho Ho. In retrospect, their names seem as weird as their constituents.)

The fruit and dessert were standard fare, but the sandwiches stood out and frequently made my friends jealous. It's worth mentioning that the bulk of my memorable and sought-after lunches were closely related to the previous night's dinner. A typical week of said lunches may have looked like this:

Meatball wedge on Monday. This meal was ideal because we prepared meatballs in a slow-cooked, homemade ragù with noodles for Sunday dinner.

Tuesday: Chicken cutlets on Italian bread or in a wedge with butter, mayo, and lettuce.

Wednesday: a wedge of eggplant Parmigiana. There was no bread with the eggplant parmigiana. It was prepared with a moderate tomato sauce, minimal cheese, and thinly sliced potatoes.

Thursday: veal cutlet sandwich or wedge with lettuce and a small amount of butter. This was back when veal was less expensive.

Friday: Scrambled eggs, pepper, and potato wedges Friday.

Because my mother's food budget was running low by the end of the week, this was an inexpensive lunch she could prepare on Thursday night after a simple dinner of pasta and salad. Weekend lunches were all about catching what you can. We would raid the fridge and make lots of peanut butter and jelly sandwiches whether or not we had friends over. We'd make tuna salad, bologna and mustard, ham and cheese, liverwurst and red onion, turkey breast and mayo, and American cheese and mayo sandwiches with whatever bread was available. We ate dill pickles, sweet gherkins, Ruffles potato chips, and Fritos. We drank gallons of milk, orange juice, apple juice, or lemonade to wash it all down (did anyone ever drink water?). We depleted the refrigerators of ice pops of every unnatural color and flavor for dessert. We did the same thing during school breaks, but in the winter, we added hot chocolate (Swiss Miss with little marshmallows from individual packets) to our gluttonous lunchtime rampages. We stuck to the same routine during the summer, like frenetic ants at an endless picnic. I don't remember anyone in our neighborhood ever taking a long summer vacation, so we just hung out for those two hot months, going from one house to the next, eating our own and each other's parents out of house and home. Summer break was my favorite time of year. The days were long, allowing us to play outside until nine p.m., at which point we would have planned an overnight at one of our houses or another, ensuring that we were never separated even while sleeping. Aside from Christmas, my favourite summer holiday is Independence Day, also known as the Fourth of July.

When I was younger, my family placed a high value on Fourth of July celebrations. All or most of my family members who had been part of the great wave of Italian immigration were still alive at the time. In comparison to the horrible poverty of the Italian south, America possessed everything that Italy could not or would not tolerate. Their dreams of a new and rich life were realized in America. They built Italian enclaves around the country by sending for relatives and friends once a job was obtained. Food was the connective tissue that kept them coming back to one other's houses, backyards, front porches, campers, beaches, and hearts. Wine lubricated any squeaky emotional wheels while also fueling any dark and dormant emotional fires. Many of these Independence Day celebrations were held at our house in northern Westchester. We'd spend days preparing for the assault by family on both sides. As more first-generation immigrants died, the Fourth of July began to lose significance. We still celebrated it, but not in the same numbers or with the same enthusiasm as before. As my generation entered early adulthood, we began to form our own political opinions, which were frequently at odds with those of many older generations, who were more conservative and continued to believe that America was the best country in the world no matter what happened. These political differences were exacerbated by the shock of 9/11. Patriotism appeared to have been monopolized by folks with hawkish views on how to right that terrible mistake, and the American flag was wielded more like a weapon than a symbol of freedom, acceptance, and possibility to me and some of my more liberal relatives. We were reverting to a country where immigrants were demonised and opposing the government's Middle Eastern conflicts was considered disloyal. Because the French refused to commit troops to fight alongside the Americans in Iraq, ultraconservatives began dubbing French fries "Freedom Fries" and boycotting and even destroying bottles of French wine. I wish they had mailed them to me. The wine, not the soldiers. As I write this, I pray that those days are coming to an end.

Chapter 2.

RETURN TO THE U.S.

My family moved from Katonah to Italy for a year in 1973 because my father had taken a vacation to study drawing, sculpting, and bronze casting at the renowned Accademia di Belle Arti in Florence. We stayed at a pensione in Rome for a couple of nights to do some sightseeing before taking the train to Florence. We visited typical historical landmarks like the Sistine Chapel, the Colosseum, and the Roman Forum, which were overwhelming to eyes that had never seen anything older than the Rockefeller Center, the Empire State Building, or a few relatives. We ate at the end of each day in a restaurant a few doors down from where we were staying, which was my first true restaurant experience. Even though I was nearly thirteen years old, the only restaurant I had been to was the Muscoot Tavern, a pizza joint a few kilometres from our house. Anyway, there were very few restaurants in that part of Westchester fifty years ago, and those that did were either diners or very expensive venues serving duck à l'orange or other French classics popular in 1970s America. With public school teachers' salaries as they were and continue to be, dining out was prohibitively expensive for a family of five, so we ate at home. Furthermore, because my mother was such an excellent cook, we could never have received anything remotely close to what she was making on any given night, even in the most famous restaurants, let alone diners. So eating at a restaurant, especially in Rome!!, was a completely new experience for my sisters and myself. When we came to Florence, I didn't know a single word of Italian, so I enrolled in an Italian school but was placed a year below where I would have normally been at my age in order to learn proper grammar alongside the other children. This proved to be an excellent decision, as I was speaking fluently within two months, and by the end of our stay, I was editing any correspondence that my father needed to write in Italian. In contrast to America, no school lunches were provided. School started around 8:00 a.m. and concluded at 1:00 p.m., when everyone went home for lunch and an afternoon sleep. To compensate for the shorter hours, we held seminars on Saturday mornings from 9:00 a.m. to 12:00 p.m. These hours were ideal because they gave me a lot more free time in the afternoons. Naturally, this arrangement was created with the expectation that there would always be an adult at home to look after the children when they arrived for lunch. Things have changed tremendously since then, but in early 1970s Italy, there was always someone in the house, usually a mother or a grandfather, at all times of day. When spring approached, having an adult present at home became even more crucial, as teacher strikes became more prevalent. There were a few faculty strikes this year, but we were usually notified if and when one was scheduled. We never learned what these impromptu walkouts were about, but as kids, we accepted them. By the time spring had arrived in full swing—the trees were in flower, the blue Italian sky soared overhead, and summer was just around the corner—the strikes had grown even more frequent and unannounced. I remember going to school multiple times and entering halls bare of personnel, with the exception of one administrator who would caution those of us wandering around asking for advice, "Ragazzi! There is no school today. There's a sciopero. "Return home!" ("Kids! Today, there is no school. There is a strike going on; "Return home!"

So we would come home. Happily. My mother, of course, questioned my unexpected return when the strikes initially started, and I joyfully explained that there was a strike. She and my father were surprised at first. They both worked at an American high school where nothing like this would ever happen. But as the instructors' absences got increasingly frequent, and I returned to the flat only a half hour after leaving, she would roll her eyes and shake her head. My sisters went to a Catholic school, and because nuns are not driven to struggle for more pay or less hours, they were educated on a regular basis. Despite learning perfect Italian, my education in Italy was virtually as good as it might have been. At this point in the chapter, I would have written about all of the meals I ate in Italy that year, but we ate at home unless we went to another city to see sites or visited relatives in Calabria. My father's salary had to be reduced for his year abroad due to the sabbatical, and although though the previous Italian lira was fairly weak in contrast to the American dollar, it still made little sense for our family to eat out. Even when we traveled across the country by train, my parents always bought all of the ingredients for sandwiches rather than paying extra to have them premade. This means that I didn't become aware of the splendour and diversity of local Italian cuisine until many years later, when I began traveling to Italy independently.

We returned to Katonah after nearly a year away, and my sisters and I were excited to see one another. We missed our friends and everything about growing up in America, especially the food. Although my mother continued to prepare healthful meals for us, we preferred peanut butter and jelly sandwiches, the occasional Swanson TV dinner on a Saturday night, a Velveeta sandwich, or frozen Buitoni "pizzas".

Peanut butter was nearly nonexistent in 1970s Italy, which may seem strange given the availability of items from almost anywhere in today's worldwide market. For those who aren't "in the know," Buitoni frozen pizzas exist (or were; are they still manufactured?). Actually, they do: small dough discs filled with a substance like tomato sauce, dried herbs, and cheese. These frozen pucks were slid directly from the freezer to the toaster, then into one's mouth. In essence, they were savory Italian-style pop tarts. We adored them. Why, you could wonder. They were the polar opposite of our typical cuisine. They made me think of Swanson TV dinners or a slab of Velveeta on white bread with mayonnaise. We craved them since it was what our friends ate. In retrospect, it's evident why my mother purchased all of these items for us, despite the fact that they were anathema to her. Yes, they were quick and easy snack foods to satisfy us, but I'd like to believe Mom purchased them to make us feel like we "belonged." However, they are more than likely to have ended up in our fridge so we could stop bothering the poor woman to buy them.

With that out of the way, here's what I ate as a teen on any given school day.

Finally, near the end of my twenties, I learned I was lactose intolerant and couldn't digest sugar properly. I immediately removed both from my diet, which provided some comfort, but the problems persisted. In brief, I experienced chronic bloating and IBS-like symptoms.

Chapter 3.

TWO DOLLARS, ONE DREAM, AND A PASTRAMI SANDWICH

After graduating from college, I moved to New York City and settled into my first apartment on 76th Street between Broadway and West End Avenue in 1982. The Upper West Side extends from 59th Street, south of Lincoln Center, to 110th Street, and from Riverside Drive to Central Park West, all of which are entirely residential, including the smaller cross streets. West End Avenue (also only residential), Broadway, Amsterdam Avenue, and Columbus Avenue are parallel to the latter two north-south highways. On these last three streets, the bottom floors of numerous apartment buildings include shops, restaurants, gyms, and other commercial establishments. For years, the Upper West Side was home to a huge number of Jewish families, as seen by the abundance of Jewish delis and bakeries. It also housed a large number of working- and middle-class families, as well as swarms of actors (especially those working in theater, as the Great White Way was only a thirty-minute walk away), many of whom lived in large rent-controlled flats. I shared a small one-bedroom apartment on the first floor with my fiancée and a college friend at the time, along with the $660 monthly rent. (Yes, we all slept in the same room; that should be the bedroom, not the bed.) The apartment had a living room, a tiny galley kitchen, a small bathroom that hadn't been updated since the mid-1960s, and the aforementioned bedroom. Because the large window overlooked an air shaft, there was minimal natural light in the living and kitchen areas. To make matters worse, this window was guarded by an accordion safety gate, which contributed to the oppressive mood. The bedroom looked out into the backs of the apartment buildings on Seventy-Fifth Street, and while it got lots of natural light, it also had a safety gate due to its proximity to the ground floor. So, effectively, apartment 2D at 107 West 76th Street was like a huge prison cell for the three of us, and we couldn't afford to stay.

Our college friend finally moved out, and shortly after that, my girlfriend and I split up, leaving me there alone. I enjoyed living alone until I experienced a prolonged spell of unemployment and found myself unable to pay the rent for one month, which had risen to more than $750. I was receiving weekly unemployment payments of around $170 and painting flats whenever I could for extra money. But this month had been a fiasco, and I was out of funds. Refusing to ask anyone for money, I went to Actors Equity and applied for money from the Actors Fund, something a colleague assured me I was entitled to do. There were no loans. It was money provided to union performers who were struggling to make ends meet. All you had to do was show that you were a current member in good standing and had consistently performed in Equity productions. I was requested to bring playbills from prior productions as well as performance ratings to verify previous work. I felt sick to my stomach at the prospect, but I was desperate. I was too proud to ask my parents for money, although knowing they would gladly give it to me. I knew that the next month I'd start working and making money, but this month I had no alternative but to swallow my pride and go begging.

The Actors' Equity office was conveniently located in Times Square, the hub of Broadway. I handed the requisite documentation to the nice gentleman behind the desk, who instantly approved the funds. I felt humiliated, humbled, but also relieved. As I stood up to leave, he inquired if I needed shoes, and I thanked him gratefully.

"Shoes?" I asked.

"Yes, shoes," he replied.

"Um, no. Why?"

"Because you are entitled to a pair, if you need them," he stated softly.

"Oh, um, no, I don't." But, thank you."

I left after he nodded and smiled.

I'm not sure if the Actors Fund developed this policy, but I found its thoughtful practicality to be very moving. Later, I realized that this free footwear offer was a relic from a time when most people only had one pair of shoes that they wore every day. If you were an actor going from audition to audition day in and day out trying to get a job, you might have worn out your shoes and needed a new pair, which is why the Actors Fund developed it.

During those few years alone in my modest apartment, I cooked pretty simple meals for myself, but I wasn't as engaged in cooking as I am now. I basically cooked pasta marinara and chicken cutlets, and I don't recall ever using the oven; everything was cooked on the small four-burner gas range. When I wasn't cooking, I ate at coffee shops, burger joints, or Cuban/Chinese restaurants (I'll get to the latter in a minute).

For roughly three dollars, one might buy a meal of fried eggs, corned beef hash, toast, home fries, orange juice, and a bottomless cup of coffee at coffee shops like John's on Sixty-Seventh Street, whose walls and cupboards still had the original white enamel of the 1930s. A soup and a sandwich, such as a bowl of split pea and grilled cheese or a turkey club, was filling and reasonable for lunch at the Cherry Restaurant, which was essentially a glorified Asian-owned coffee shop with a full Chinese menu. Dinner was generally at a burger establishment like Big Nick's, which served gigantic, greasy, bloody burgers on fat buns that I still crave to this day. (I'm salivating just thinking about the goddamn things as I write this.) After that heart-stopping repast, whether alone or with friends, I would see a movie for approximately two dollars or go to the bowling alley on Seventy-Sixth and Amsterdam, which had somehow remained intact since the 1940s. I'd come here to drink Budweiser or Miller High Life beer from long-neck bottles, eat American cheese sandwiches on white bread after having eaten nearly half a cow an hour before, bowl the night away, and never spend more than ten pieces of the big bourgeois long green. The Upper West Side, like the West Village, has a substantial gay community, with several independently owned and run gay pubs and restaurants on Amsterdam and Columbus Avenues. Unfortunately, gentrification took hold in the mid- and late-1980s, and many buildings were converted into condominiums and co-ops or simply demolished to make way for new, poorly planned housing for the up-and-coming at costs that most people could not afford. Gentrification's increasing rents also coincided with the AIDS crisis, causing many gay-owned companies to close just as the disease took the lives of many of those who owned them and decimated the ranks of their dedicated consumers.

As the neighbourhood's profile became less diverse in every manner, the individual businesses that supported the residents and gave the region its distinct flavour became homogenised, as has so much of America. Old coffee shops like Jones and the Cherry Restaurant vanished one by one, rapidly replaced by a Starbucks or some variation thereof. Independently owned hardware and clothing stores were supplanted by large chains, as were independently held pharmacies, shoe stores, booksellers, and barbershops, many of which had interiors that had not altered since the 1930s and 1940s. The lovely vintage WWII-era bowling alley was dismantled and replaced with a crudely furnished "upscale" pool hall. Many small eateries that reflected the neighbourhood's unique ethnic and cultural profile were also eliminated. There were a number of Jewish delicatessens that featured traditional delicacies such as matzo ball soup, potato latkes, pastrami sandwiches (but none as delicious as those from the now-defunct Carnegie Deli), and marble babke. To that end, let us leave the Upper West Side for a few minutes and travel about twenty blocks downtown to grieve the loss of the aforementioned Gan Eden of delicatessens. The Carnegie Deli opened in 1937 and quickly became a favourite of both New Yorkers and tourists. If a restaurant in a city is discovered and frequented by visitors, native patrons will usually go elsewhere. This was not the situation at the Carnegie Deli. Native New Yorkers may have gone at odd hours when the never-ending line to enter had vanished and the dining room wasn't so crowded that it appeared to be a firetrap, but they still went. And the point is, it was impossible not to go there. Yes, the cuisine was wonderful, but it was also a way to catch a taste of old New York while so much of the city was reinventing itself over and over again. If I had a meeting, an audition, or was performing on Broadway, I would frequently stop by the Carnegie Deli for a bowl of chicken soup (with noodles and matzo balls, please, I'll have both) and a tower of pastrami sandwiches. Every Jewish deli serves massive portions of beef, chicken, or tuna salad between two slices of bread. (Please watch the wonderful comedy stylings of Nick Kroll and John Mulaney doing their hilarious sketches in coffee shops centred on "too much tuna! " on YouTube. Your life will be altered in a positive way.) The Carnegie Deli, on the other hand, went overboard. Their motto was "If you've finished your meal, we've done something wrong." Despite the fact that the sandwiches were gigantic and that practically anyone would have struggled to get the mammoth of rye and still-warm pastrami in their mouth, let alone complete one, you were not permitted to split a single order. So a friend and I would split a sandwich, eat as much as we could, and then take the rest home for a midnight snack. If I was really hungry, I'd get the Frisbee-size latkes with applesauce on the side. While I waited for my food, I would drink a beer or a cream soda and nibble on the pickles floating in the small stainless-steel bowl of room-temperature brine that rested on each table. I preferred the half-sour pickles while looking for my catch; I tried not to think about when the murky liquid had last been refilled or how many hands before mine had fished about for "just the right one." If I was feeling very Chekhovian, I would have the borscht instead of the chicken soup on occasion. Everything was good. Everything was wonderful. The meal at the Carnegie Deli warmed you up after a night at a Broadway theatre or a dance performance at City Center, just a couple of windswept blocks away. When you popped in late at night after a few too many at a cheap downtown pub, en route to the one-bedroom apartment you believed you'd be living in for the rest of your life if you didn't get a job soon, it covered your tummy and comforted your spirit.

But, like so many other magnificent old New York City restaurants and pubs, the Carnegie Deli is no longer in business. (To be honest, Carnegie's demise was not because the rent was raised or the building was demolished; it was because the second-generation owner decided she'd had enough, which is her right but a terrible loss for all of us.)

However, as I previously stated, gentrification in New York has resulted in the closure of numerous enterprises that had no wish to close, as well as the demolition of far too many structures and culturally significant sites to count. (A great example is the old Penn Station, which was violently demolished after serving the city for only sixty years.) I'm not sure why, but we Americans feel little need to maintain what previously was because we perceive it as less than what is or could be. We haven't yet learnt, like children and adolescents, that the present isn't the only thing. Obviously, change is good, but there is no reason to erase the past while developing the future. They can and should live together. Wonderful venues have closed, including Lüchow's, Gage & Tollner, I, and the Oyster Bar at the Plaza Hotel, as well as newer ones like Elaine's, Kiev, and Florent. Almost always, the primary reason for their downfall is financial. Either the rent has been raised, the economy has tanked, the owner has refused to allow the employees to unionise, or they have just fallen out of favour. Although times and preferences have changed, their menus and décor have not. If they could have hung on for a little longer, a new generation would have rediscovered their classic cuisine and old-world charm and brought them back to life. Of course, there are still a few ancient restaurants around the city, such as Delmonico's, Peter Luger, Fraunces Tavern, the ancient Homestead, and Barbetta, but considering the city's physical size and population of over 8 million people, it is a pittance. There are dozens in Paris, which has a population of 2.2 million people.

Who would we be if our grandparents and parents had not treasured and passed down their family history in the shape of clothing, furniture, crockery, silverware, books, photos, artwork, diaries, and so on? These souvenirs do not need to be of high monetary value; only emotional value is required. I have my mother's pots and pans that I will never part with, not only because "nobody makes them like that anymore," but also because they remind me of her and the great meals she prepared for our family. Losing a treasured family heirloom is a profound personal loss; these are items that can never be reproduced or recreated. Family recipes, on the other hand, may be the most valuable heirlooms. They serve as physical heirlooms, reminding us of where we originated from and telling others, in a bite, the narrative of another people from another location and another time. Unlike a lost physical relic, however, recipes are a part of our history that may be recreated time and again. They can only be lost if we want to lose them. I understand that growth is good for business and that business is business, but the casual destruction of great restaurants and their classic foods derived from historic recipes that helped shape a city is a huge loss for any culture, no matter how you slice it. And if you cut as much of it as a decent Jewish deli, especially as much as the Carnegie used to, that is a startling loss.

Let's take a walk back to the Upper West Side now. As we travel north these days, we will see that the gastronomic landscape is considerably different from what I encountered over forty years ago. Columbus Circle is currently dominated by a massive structure that houses the Mandarin Oriental, a jazz performance venue, offices, and apartments, as well as an expensive mall and numerous eateries. You can eat at any of them if you have a lot of money, but only if you've recently robbed a bank can you dine at Per Se, where supper starts at $355 for a nine-course tasting menu sans wine. That is, as I already stated, without wine. There is no wine included. There is no wine pairing with your $325 tasting menu. However, if you want to save money by bringing your own wine, there is a $150 corkage cost per bottle. Just keep in mind that an 8.875 percent sales tax is not included. Neither is the wine, as I believe I indicated. A steal if there ever was one. I've never eaten there, but I've heard it's fantastic.

We continue north, passing by Jean-Georges Vongerichten's eponymous restaurant in the Trump International Hotel, which is as good as its landlord is evil. As we proceed up Broadway, we notice that numerous good but expensive restaurants have appeared in the last two decades, among corporate retailers such as the Gap, Brooks Brothers, Pottery Barn, and 117 Starbucks. Finally, on 78th Street, we come across La Caridad, a fifty-year-old jewel of a restaurant.

La Caridad, one of Manhattan's last remaining Cuban-Chinese eateries, was founded in the late 1960s by Rafael Lee, a Chinese immigrant who first migrated to Cuba and then to the United States, and is now owned by his son. It serves a strange and delightful mix of Cuban and Chinese dishes at extremely low prices. If you're not from New York, you might be wondering, "What, why, and how Cuban-Chinese?" " The truth is that many Chinese migrated to Cuba in the mid-1800s to work on railroads, then again around the turn of the century and later when Chairman Mao came to power. Many Cuban-Chinese escaped communism and moved to New York during the start of the Cuban Revolution, where they built restaurants that served dishes inspired by their dual ancestry.

My first apartment was only two blocks from La Caridad, so I was frequently spotted at its tables. There were often a few cabs loitering on the street outside, their drivers devouring the restaurant's food from takeaway containers, because they, like the rest of us, knew the food was delicious, the service was lightning fast, and the pricing was ridiculously low. The restaurant looks almost like a terrarium, with big glass windows looking out onto Broadway and 79th.

To begin, a wonton soup may be ordered, followed by an oxtail stew or shrimp fried rice as a complement to ropa vieja, or pulled beef in a rich brown sauce. As I recall, a slightly oily but wonderful fried chicken (mainly dark meat) with a side of yellow rice, red or black beans, fried plantains, and an avocado-and-onion salad would cost between $6 and $8. Obviously, costs have risen over the last four decades, but they remain relatively fair. It was one of the rare Cuban-Chinese restaurants with an espresso machine years ago, and while the coffee wasn't quite as they make it in Rome, it was a nice break from the acidic dishwater that passed for java at most of the coffee shops around. A large oval plate of shrimp with yellow rice, peas, and a side of black beans could fill a young actor for several hours at La Caridad, until he became hungry again and was forced to make himself yet another dinner of pasta marinara washed down with the remains of a cheap bottle of red, because he had spent his allotment of cash for the day. But he knew in his heart of hearts and gut of stomachs that it had been worthwhile. When I visit New York, I go to the Upper West Side, a neighbourhood I was happy to be a part of for so many years when I dressed as a younger guy. As I previously stated, it has altered dramatically, both for the better and for the worst. It's safer and cleaner, but so much of the past's texture has been gone. I still make a point of eating at La Caridad, not just because I enjoy it, but also because all of the other Cuban-Chinese restaurants within a twenty-block radius have closed. Their square footage has been converted into soulless cafés dominated by tattooed baristas who ask for your first name so they can write it on your eco-cup and then yell it for everyone to hear when your order is ready. Today, one may buy a cup of coffee for the price of a hearty meal provided with an interesting slice of ethnic culinary history on the side in these types of establishments.

Chapter 4.

SALT, BUTTER, AND THE SHAPE OF MEMORY

My late wife, Kathryn Spath, and I married in 1995 after four years of dating. She was a mother with two young children at the time. In 2000, we got twins Nicolo and Isabel, and in 2002, we welcomed our daughter Camilla. She died four years later, in 2009, at the age of 47, having been diagnosed with stage four breast cancer in 2005. She was an excellent mother, wife, and friend. She was intelligent, beautiful, kind, and patient, and one of the best people I've ever encountered. I loved her and will continue to do so. Her death, like her absence, is unfathomable to me. Kate, like me, valued good food, as demonstrated by our first date at Tout Va Bien, a modest French restaurant in Manhattan. It opened in 1948 and, happily, is still operational. We both ordered their always-delicious coq au vin, and I'm pretty sure Kate finished hers, half a baguette, and a couple glasses of wine before I even got started on mine. When I first met her, she was a single mother who managed a childcare company out of her home to supplement her income. Despite this, she cooked a well-balanced meal and had a proper sit-down dinner with her children every night, no matter how tired she was from a hard day. The meals were largely simple and kid-friendly, but they were varied and nutritious, and both of her children developed into good eaters as a result. When I joined the family, Kate and I naturally started cooking together, and the number and variety of dishes we cooked grew over time. I began incorporating my family's dishes into our daily meals, and Kate, like my wife, Felicity, consistently outperformed me. Some of them are vastly superior.

I recall Kate making my mother's recipe for lasagna Bolognese, a family favorite, shortly before she was diagnosed. Handmade plain and spinach pasta is layered in a baking dish with Bolognese sauce, besciamella, and grated Parmigiano. As a result, the dish is both outrageously rich and delicate, and no one who consumes it appears to be able to stop eating. Needless to say, it is really tough to get right. The pasta must be the right thickness, just thick enough to hold its structure and absorb the sauce while staying thin enough to virtually melt in your mouth after a single bite. The Bolognese sauce should not be very meaty, as this would make it too heavy, and it should also have the proper amounts of carrots, celery, onion, and tomato to offer the appropriate sweetness. The besciamella cannot be too runny or "claggy," as they say in the UK, and everything must be assembled with care to avoid damaging the pasta sheets. In conclusion, if you have the time and patience, give it a try. If you don't, just don't. You will make yourself and everyone else unhappy.

Kate had been experimenting with this recipe for years and had had excellent success, but she was often asking my mother for advice or recommendations on how to improve it. My mother is extremely patient and supportive when teaching people how to cook, yet she can be intimidating owing to her extensive knowledge, experience, and expertise. But, as usual, Kate appeared unconcerned. Because the recipe was time-consuming and labor-intensive, it was typically served on special occasions. One day, just my parents, Kate, my stepdaughter Christine, the little kids, and I were celebrating something; I'm not sure what it was, but it was certainly special enough for Kate to prepare this rare gastronomic delicacy. As we all tucked in, it became evident that she had outdone herself. While my father and I were sighing with delight, I noticed my mother eating slowly, her eyes focused as if she was trying to enter every last taste bud with the flavors of what she had just eaten. After a brief moment, Kate looked at her and bravely asked, "What do you think, Joanie?"

My mother continued to chew calmly, her gaze fixated on the plate. After a brief, uncomfortable time, she turned to Kate and said, "I have nothing left to teach you." Then she began crying.

Kate was overjoyed when she wrapped her arms around my mother. The rest of us broke into laughter. The lasagna was then eaten. Eating with my in-laws, Kate's mother Dorothy and her second husband Brad, was a vastly different experience than eating with my parents. Although I like visiting them, they were not necessarily a cooking couple. They enjoyed dining, as do many others, but the prospect of cooking something other than baked chicken or steak, or experimenting with new dishes, sparked their interest. Some people enjoy cooking, while others do not, and our visits were always enjoyable.

Dorothy and Brad lived on a nice property on the Maine coast in Freeport, an ancient town now primarily made up of outlet stores such as L.L.Bean and Sebago. Kate and I, together with my stepchildren and, eventually, our children, would travel five hours north from Westchester to visit most summers. We'd cruise out on their little boat to different islands, go for hikes in the woods, or spend hours shopping at Freeport's big L.L. Bean store for things we didn't need like polar fleeces, thermoses, and carabiners. During our visits, Kate and I would always do the cooking because we knew what our kids would and wouldn't eat, cooking made us happy, and being cooked made my in-laws happy. But there was one supper Brad made that Kate and I would never try.

Brad was born and bred in Maine, yet he still used the flat tones that "Maniacs" are known for. For those who have never visited Maine, it is a beautiful, mountainous state with short summers and long, harsh winters. Anyone who was not born in Maine is classified as a "outsider," regardless of how long they have lived there. They are generally quiet folks with a sharp, bone-dry sense of humour. Here's an illustration of a Maine comedic pun: When I was trying to strike up a conversation with a member of a local "yacht club," I inquired whether he had lived in Maine his entire life. He responded with a deadpan, "Not yet." Following that, the discussion quickly subsided.

However, one ritual that tends to scrape the aristocratic barnacles off even the most stoic of the state's citizens is eating lobster picked from Maine's ever-frigid coastal waters with friends and family. The effort required by everyone at the table to accurately dissect a steamed lobster prompts the participants to help one another complete the assignment. This act tears down all barriers and is sure to spark debate. I've eaten lobster in England, the Maldives, Ireland, and numerous other locations, but nothing compares to a one-and-a-half-pound Maine lobster. I am not a fan of grilled, thermidor, or Newburged lobster, no matter how good it is. I'm not saying I don't like lobster bisque or lobster rolls on lightly toasted, buttered buns. When it comes to fresh lobster, I believe they should be gently boiled in salted water with simply butter, preferably clarified, added to enrich the flavor. Every summer, Brad cooked them on the beach of a little island off the coast of Maine.

Brad would check the weather forecast the day before we arrived and decide what would be the best time for our annual island/lobster adventure. We'd pack coolers with beer, water, and soda, as well as hunks of cheese and homemade smoked salmon pâté, stuff plastic bags with ears of corn and loaves of bread, gather life jackets, and head down to the rocky shore that the house overlooked. Brad carried a damaged and burnt aluminum pot, a little wire shelf from a broken fridge, and a stash of firewood in two old burlap bags. We'd then all board a tiny dinghy and row to the motorboat, which was anchored about fifty yards away. We'd board the boat and proceed to a nearby marina, where Brad knew a lobsterman who offered perfect-size lobsters for a low price. The crabs were placed in an empty cooler and hurried onto our boat, their quick, lethal claws rendered ineffective by taut elastic bands.

We would pass seal harems swimming and sunning themselves on the jagged charcoal-colored rocks as we made our way through the freezing blue water toward a little island with a less difficult beach than the majority of the other nearby islands. The entire location was a New England idyll suitable for any Wyeth family member. We'd anchor the boat off the island, then board the dinghy and row to shore.

I make it sound easy, but there was always a lot of cursing and swearing about improperly tied mooring lines, uneven weight distribution, how many trips it would take to get us all ashore, who would go first, and the designated rower's insufferable inability to row in a straight line. However, as we landed on the island, the sound of tabs being hastily removed from chilled beer cans served to calm us considerably. While Kate and her mother set out the hors d'oeuvres, Brad, the kids, and I would gather stones and form a circle to contain the fire. We started a fire with the wood Brad had brought and some dried pine branches picked from the island, balanced the old freezer grate on the stones above the flames, and waited for it to burn evenly. We filled the aluminium pot with seawater and placed it on the grate over the now-roaring fire after a few minutes. When the water came to a boil, the lobsters were gently placed in it and covered with seaweed. The young people shucked the sweet corn and placed it on top of the seaweed, which was then covered with more seaweed. While we ate cheese and crackers and waited for our Maine course, butter melted in a tiny kettle next to the fire. (The pun was intended and performed.)

I'm not sure how Brad knew when the lobsters were done; he never timed them. He seemed to just know. And he was always right. The meat we took from the shells was consistently well cooked. We dipped it enthusiastically into the melted butter before slathering cold butter on top of the hot corn and finished with a sprinkle of salt.

Butter and salt.

Salt and butter.

Those two condiments enhanced the flavors of an ancient plant and a prehistoric aquatic decapod, resulting in a breathtakingly magnificent experience for all of us. As I previously indicated, this was Brad's first dinner other than a burger or a steak on the grill, and we were all grateful that he had concentrated his efforts on mastering it, since it was great.

If fresh seaweed was available, Kate and I always prepared lobster using Brad's tried-and-true method, which I still do to this day. However, I'm still far from Kate's recurrent successes with lasagna alla Bolognese, but I'm working on it. Felicity will most likely do this before I leave the gate.

Chapter 5.

MERRY CHRISTMAS! (AND OTHER WARNINGS)

Every year, as the days grow shorter in England, where I now live, I can't help but recall the winters of my youth in upper Westchester, New York, which occurred more than 50 years ago. Our house was located on a cul-de-sac at the top of a hill, surrounded by trees that were almost usually covered in snow by early December. The ponds and lakes would begin to freeze over, and the woodlands around us would transform into studies in hard black and soft white, making them even more enigmatic and appealing than before. I liked everything about winter, especially Christmas. Our Chrlstmases were happy experiences that I still aspire to recreate now. Despite my parents' limited financial resources, they made certain that our home was always tastefully decorated. My father had created a modernist manger out of walnut wood scraps, which included contemporary figurines of Mary, Joseph, and the Christ child. Other, more generic store-bought replicas of shepherds, wise men, and farm animals made their way into our Gropius-inspired stable throughout the years, but they always felt like unsophisticated intruders. Each year, when this homemade "presepio" (Italian for "creche"), the Christmas tree lights (the big, primary-colored, hand-painted variety), the stockings, and other ornamental holiday bric-a-brac were freed from their crumbling cardboard boxes, I felt an almost unbearable rush of joy. I knew Christmas would take us out of our routine and into a week or so of unstructured days full of boundless play.

We are solely fish on Christmas Eve as an Italian Catholic family, despite our lack of practice. Our typical menu consisted of prepared food from recipes passed down through generations, but during Christmas, this practice was elevated to even greater traditional culinary heights. The tradition of feeding fish on Christmas Eve is considered to have arisen from the Roman practice of refraining from eating meat the night before a feast day. This feast is known as the Feast of the Seven Fishes in certain households, but no one knows why there are seven, other than the fact that it is the most commonly used number in Scripture. When I was a kid, my family prepared at least seven different types of fish for Christmas Eve.

The main dinner followed the cod and other first-course items (there were so many that I once suggested my parents build a vomitorium). This was frequently grilled bluefish.

Bluefish is not commonly eaten since most people find it greasy and "fishy." (It's less oily than mackerel and has lighter, flakier meat, but it's from the same family. Both of these characteristics, however, are mitigated if it is cooked correctly. It's also a touch bony, which always put me off as a kid, but the flavor was so amazing that I'd pick my way through my share with my bony little hands, much to my parents' dismay.

This dish requires minimal preparation. The fish is cut in half lengthwise and liberally seasoned with breadcrumbs, olive oil, minced garlic, chopped parsley, and salt before being topped with a few thinly sliced lemon rounds. It is then placed on a baking pan, covered loosely with foil, and baked at 325 degrees Fahrenheit. After about 20 to 30 minutes, remove the foil and turn the oven to broil (grill if you are British, which is still funny to me to this day), and cook the fish for about five minutes to crisp and brown the top before allowing it to rest for a few minutes.

As you may be aware, cooking fish causes your kitchen to smell like... fish. Cooking bluefish will intensify its fishy aroma. Not like rotten fish, but just... more. Don't let it dissuade you from giving it a try! I promise that the delicate breadcrumb mixture and the acidity of the lemon combine wonderfully to balance out the pungency of this particular toxin, giving it an almost sweet flavor.

My father and I would take turns hosting Christmas Eve and Christmas Day over the years. If I were hosting Christmas Eve, I would make some of the previously mentioned appetizers, but because I don't have the time, or even the desire, to match my mother's stunning output, I would simply make a massive pot of fish stew with at least seven different types of shellfish. I'd serve it with toasted bread or as a sauce for pasta, typically spaghetti or linguine. It remains one of my favourite recipes to prepare for company. The beauty of it is that almost any type of seafood can be utilized, with the exception of highly oily fish like mackerel, sardines, and salmon. It takes no time to prepare and, unless you are allergic to shellfish, is always a hit. Serving fish on Christmas Eve is not a tradition in England, but I still prepare at least two or three fish dishes that night. They are, in my opinion, a necessary moderate precursor to the approaching meat-heavy Christmas and Boxing Day feasts. Christmases spent with my in-laws in England are like many others I've had in my life. The day is filled with gift-giving, wine-pouring, game-playing, and, for the first time in my life, Christmas-cracker pulling. The cuisine, on the other hand, differs the most from my family's Christmas Day menu, but it is just as delicious, thanks to my mother-in-law Joanna's exceptional cooking skills. Hors d'oeuvres include "devils on horseback" (dates wrapped in bacon and cooked to a light crisp) and small sausages that disappear down our throats in seconds on miniature rivers of champagne. Unlike an Italian lunch, there is no first course (please see the following chapter for more information), and the food is plentiful: Roasted potatoes, steaming vegetables, and bread sauce, a mush-like dish. (Bread sauce is milk-soaked white bread that resembles and tastes like something Mr. Bumble and his ilk would have fed to workhouse lads or toothless Victorian old. Everything else is fine, but it isn't my favorite.)

All of these are served alongside the main course, which is always an exquisite piece of meat. Years ago, it was normally a turkey, but since my arrival and the addition of an American Thanksgiving to the calendar, we've all agreed that two turkeys in a month is a little repetitive on the palate. As a result, the main course is either a three-bird roast (known as a turducken in America) consisting of a deboned chicken stuffed within a deboned duck, which is then stuffed inside a deboned turkey or goose; a baked ham; a standing rib of beef; or a large fat goose all on its own. I adore them all, as does everyone else at the table, so there is very little left over at the conclusion of the meal. On my first British Yuletide, I discovered the renowned English Christmas Day treat sticky toffee pudding, which was both novel and delicious. I'm not a great fan of sweets, but this one is difficult to pass up, especially with a glass of fine port that my father-in-law generously provides at the end of the supper. We're all stuffed after this feast, and listening to my family's British accents makes me wonder what Christmas might have been like here in the past. I imagine myself putting on my frock coat and top hat, wrapping my long woollen scarf around my neck, bidding my in-laws farewell, and strolling home with my family through snowy streets lined with Georgian homes, the smoke of the coal fires within wafting from their chimneys as we make our way to the Cratchit house to check on dear sweet Tiny Tim once more. When I open the front door of my in-laws' house and discover that it is raining again, or still, my Hollywood vision of Jolly Old England is shattered. The kids are crying because they are leaving their grandparents, apparently forever in their minds, and we make our way into the driveway, wrestle them into their car seats while the older kids squeeze into any empty space available, and carefully drive the one mile back home before Emilia, two, vomits all over herself due to her chronic car sickness. Let's discuss Dickensian.

Christmas Day

Christmas mornings with three tiny children are both joyful and exhausting, as any parent with three small children knows. Kate and I would have to stop the kids from attacking their gifts as velociraptors do when they get up too early. I always kept huge plastic bags on hand and would fill them with shredded wrapping paper as soon as it was ripped from the gifts by their nervous little hands. (This is to ensure that tidiness is maintained and that no gifts are accidentally misplaced or abandoned beneath what will soon be mountains of paper. I once threw away a gorgeous antique pencil drawing I had bought as a gift for Kate, and I've been following the "unwrap—grab the wrap—bag the wrap" strategy ever since. Since then, no piece of artwork or tin toy soldier has been lost.

After all of the commotion and excitement of gift-giving had subsided, and some adult relative who had come to stay was assembling a toy that I refused to assemble because I can't stand reading instructions, our plan was always to lounge around in our pjs, sip coffee, and watch the kids short-circuit as they bounced from one toy to the next. Every year, we imagined that these rare moments of calm would be achievable because guests did not arrive until midafternoon for Christmas dinner. However, this does not occur on an annual basis. The explanation behind this is as follows.

On Christmas Day, a particularly special dish is served in our home. It is known as timpano. A cooked pastry-like dough drum stuffed with spaghetti, ragù, salami, cheeses, hard-boiled eggs, and meatballs. It's a large, hearty dish that will definitely fill you up. My father's family brought the recipe and the tradition of serving it on important occasions, such as Christmas, to America. I never recall not eating it on Christmas Day, whether we were at our house or the home of one of my father's siblings. It's such a showstopper that we decided to feature it in Big Night as the centerpiece of the film's final feast. However, both its preparation and cooking require a significant amount of time and effort. For this reason, even though we wouldn't be eating until two or three p.m., my parents would arrive around eleven a.m. to begin the process of finishing the timpano, which they had diligently prepared a couple of days prior.

When I heard the sound of automobile tires on the gravel drive, I'd gaze at Kate sheepishly, followed by my parents' yells of "Merry Christmas!" She'd sigh lightly before slowly turning and staring at me, and I could feel something die in her eyes. My anxiety would skyrocket at this point, and I'd rush to the bar to see if I could find liquid comfort in a bloody Mary or a scotch sour. My nicely dressed parents would ascend the stairs smiling from ear to ear, as if we'd been apart for decades, despite the fact that we'd only seen them the night before, laden with gifts and platters of food,III included the pièce de résistance, covered in a huge dishcloth. They were so happy and eager, I couldn't imagine being annoyed by their early arrival. (Perhaps not me, but my poor wife.) I will show you how. The timpano is an instrument.

First, let me give you the recipe so you can become acquainted with this classic Tucci family meal.

A yule epilogue

Felicity Blunt, my wife, and I started dating in the fall of 2010 (more details in a later chapter), and she moved to Westchester approximately a year later to be with me and the kids. I hoped Felicity would react differently to Timpano than Kate did during her first Christmas with us. That did not happen. What happened was exactly as described in the previous pages. I am not joking. Exactly. The inevitable late-night talk begins with the words, now spoken darkly in a posh British accent: "That fucking timpano..."

Chapter 6.

SECONDO'S SILENCE

Making a cooking show or a food documentary for television requires incredibly specialized talents, energy, and skill sets, which I have gradually mastered over the years. Making a fictitious narrative film in which food is key is a very new ballgame, and doing so (although badly) transformed my life dramatically. Over thirty years ago, I started writing what would become the film Big Night. I'd always wanted to write a script that captured the tone and structure of a "foreign film." By this, I mean a film that concentrated mostly on the characters, avoided stereotypes, and ended ambiguously. When I lived on Manhattan's Upper West Side in the 1980s, I was frequently unemployed for long periods of time. Instead of sitting at home waiting for the phone to ring, I would exercise, visit museums, go to the theatre (cheap standing-room tickets only), or see a movie. In contrast to today, there were many privately owned cinemas that showed international and independent films. After finishing my daily workout, I ate an inexpensive, very unhealthy dinner at the nearby coffee shop (which is no longer there), grabbed a cup of coffee to go, paid my few bucks, and sat in a half-empty theatre to watch the magnificent Babette's Feast.

If you haven't watched the film yet, I highly recommend it, especially if you're a "foodie." To avoid spoilers, I distinctly recall hearing the audience sigh with unmet delight as each dish was presented during the climax dinner sequence. There is no doubt that the sounds pouring from the cinema during Babette's Feast were only heard in Times Square cinemas exhibiting films of a far different caliber. (At least, it is what I have been informed.) In any case, the film's subtle brilliance and shared viewing experience stayed with me for many years, eventually inspiring Big Night. Any number of experiences might inspire or influence what someone does, but the most significant inspiration for Big Night was an Italian restaurant in Miami that I visited while filming early in my career. It was managed by two immigrant brothers, one of whom would frequently sing while serving you. Although I can't recall the brothers' names or the name of the restaurant, I remember them as charming raconteurs who served delicious food. During the same trip, I met a Corsican named Pascal, who had the air of a wannabe mafioso and ran another popular Italian restaurant. This stunning, blue-eyed, foul-mouthed restaurateur served as the model for Ian Holm's depiction of Pascal in Big Night. The brothers of the aforementioned diner prompted Tony Shalhoub and me to play Primo and Secondo, respectively.

However, one incident I had as a young man inspired the film's setting in a restaurant. My objective was to work and live in Manhattan between my sophomore and junior years of college. Fortunately, because to familial generosity and old-fashioned nepotism, I was able to get a job at Alfredo's, the Original of Rome, in midtown. My uncle Frank, my father's brother, planned the decor for Alfredo's and persuaded the management to engage me, while my aunt Dora and her husband, Bob, graciously accommodated me in their spare bedroom in their gorgeous East Side apartment. I could not have been fortunate or happier. So, at the age of 19, I started working as a busboy at Alfredo's. However, because I spoke English, was a lousy busboy, or both, I was quickly promoted to "bar boy".

Alfredo's did a lot of lunch business, primarily from local entrepreneurs and travelers looking for authentic Italian cuisine. I use the term "authentic" since Alfredo's was a sister restaurant of Alfredo's in Rome. As one might guess, the signature dish was fettuccine Alfredo. Alfredo di Lelio created this now-ubiquitous dish in 1907. It's just fettuccine with butter and Parmigiano-Reggiano. Not fundamentally; it is just that. But Alfredo's version, with a bit more butter and Parmigiano, as well as the sight of it being cooked tableside, with the long strands of fettuccine glistening with the fats of the butter and cheese, became an international sensation. Whoever held the name saw an opportunity to operate in New York in the late 1970s, and the establishment is still in business today, serving the titular dish according to the original recipe. However, the sublimely simple combination of butter and cheese has been adjusted to match American tastes in various places over the years. Cream has penetrated (unneeded), as has chicken (yuck), broccoli (why?), and turkey (really?). F*** off). Anyway, fettuccine Alfredo was pretty much all I ate this summer, and as a college student, I thought it was fantastic.

At Alfredo's, the bartender did more than just make drinks; he also poured wine and made espresso and cappuccino. For nearly three hours, I was constantly distributing liquids from one vessel to another while also reloading glasses, ice, fruit, garnishes, coffee grinds, milk, and so on. And I really enjoyed it. Cleaning and organizing not only satisfy and comfort me, but they also allow me to reflect about topics like how I may approach a particular vocation or whether anyone will ever hire me again. So I was in OCD heaven: scrubbing a bar, organizing a stockroom, and being paid for it. I was told by two different chain-smoking bartenders. The first was a sharp-witted Albanian who, like many of his compatriots, spoke Italian. The other was a former marine, mercenary army, and ex-convict from the United States who had served time in prison for murder. (I believe he was eventually released because his crime was classified as self-defense, or something similar. But, in any event, he killed someone, which I found terrifyingly cool at the time. Needless to say, I was very careful not to irritate him. So the homicidal mercenary and the silver-tongued Albanian took me under their nicotine-stained wings and gradually taught me how to be a very fluid, efficient bartender, a skill I aim to regain, and I will be eternally grateful to them.

Alfredo's, like many eateries, was a whirlwind of energy emanating from a cultural melting pot of employees. Coming from Westchester's mostly white suburbs, it was refreshing to be a part of an organization with the same ethnic diversity as the United Nations. Except for a couple of native New Yorkers whose origins I never discovered, the waiters were Greek, Egyptian, Italian, Albanian, Spanish, and Eastern European, while the majority of the kitchen and bus staff were Puerto Rican or Dominican. As a young actor, I admired the range of accents and the unintentional beauty that occurred when someone had to convey what they were thinking in one language to another. I was also fascinated by how the structure of a restaurant resembled that of a theatre. The kitchen was "backstage," and during a lunch or dinner rush, it was its own strange biosphere, populated by frantic humans barely controlling flames and swords. Simultaneously, the eating area was "onstage," where some of the same people immediately became cool, calm, and collected, almost to the point of being benign, after passing through a swinging door. I've only ever seen and, of course, demonstrated this crazy behavior while performing in a theater. It's both interesting and sad because it's not only common, but also essential in certain situations.

Many years later, when I was finally able to support myself entirely through acting and no longer needed to work in restaurants or paint apartments, I began to dwell on these occurrences and decided to put them down in a screenplay-like format. After a few years of getting nowhere fast, I approached my first cousin and one of my best friends, Joseph Tropiano, who shared my interest in cinema. Over the next five years or so, we gradually arrived at something we were satisfied with. It was a screenplay that dramatized the conflict between commerce and art, portrayed the Italian immigrant as unrelated to the Mafia (an unusual portrayal in American cinema), demonstrated the importance of food in Italian culture and how it is frequently used to express emotions, and did not have a happy ending. We had no clue we were making something that would be so well received or that it would become a "food film" cult favorite. We could have negotiated a better back end if we had understood any of it. Campbell Scott, Co-Director of Big Night, introduced me to Isabella Rossellini. Isabella agreed to star in the film while we circulated the script to every Christian producer. I mentioned to Isabella that I wanted to spend some time with a chef at work, and she recommended Pino Luongo, a New York City restaurateur. After I explained what I was looking for, Pino recommended that I visit Le Madri, one of his restaurants on Seventeenth and Seventh Avenue, where Gianni Scappin was the head chef.

Gianni Scappin is from Mason Vicentino, a small village in Northern Italy's Veneto area, where his family owned a little restaurant. Gianni realized he was not cut out for the priesthood after a brief stint in a seminary school as a young child, and at the age of fourteen, he began a four-year course at the Recoaro Terme Culinary Institute, which increased his expertise of Italian regional dishes. He moved to England at the age of eighteen and honed his classic cooking skills in the French-influenced kitchen of the Dorset Hotel in Bournemouth. He worked at the famed Hotel Excelsior on the Lido in Venice after completing a two-year required stint in the Italian army in an Alpine skiing unit, where he also cooked for his commanding officers (enlist now). In the early 1980s, he spent a few years as head chef at New York's extremely successful Castellano before going on to Bice (where he taught the late, great Anthony Bourdain) and, finally, Le Madri. He eventually left the kitchen to manage Pino Luongo's five New York restaurants. He left the city in 2000 to open his own restaurants in upstate New York, and he taught at the CIA's Colavita Center for Italian Food and Wine (not the actual espionage organization).

Gianni could not have been more welcoming, and even though I had the opportunity to see some of Pino's other kitchens, I never left Le Madri after meeting Gianni. As we sought funding for the film over the next three years, whenever I wasn't working, I'd spend time in Gianni's kitchen, learning everything I could from the crew and picking his brain. I asked Gianni to show me how to make a frittata because at the end of the film, my character, Secondo, makes one and shares it with his brother, Primo, and the busboy/waiter, Cristiano. Our bold goal was to film the scenario in a single, uninterrupted take with no coverage. This meant that there would be no way to reduce it down, therefore every part had to work perfectly, which required me to be really talented at building it. There is also no conversation, with the exception of a few phrases at the beginning, making it feel almost like a silent film scene. Because I was filming the scenario in a single wide master shot, I had to make the frittata in real time. If something went wrong, I'd have to trim, reset, and start again.

We rehearsed multiple times to finalise the performers' blocking and overall timing. During rehearsal, I used a pan borrowed from the prop master. It was or appeared to be a late 1950s pan, so there was no way of slipping in a Teflon-coated pan to make my task easier. Needless to say, the frittata was sticking to the pan, and I started to worry because if it didn't work out, we'd have to shoot coverage and edit the sequence. We all instinctively knew that doing so would risk the scene's emotional integrity and remove its suspense. So I bought a large aluminum pan and gave it a shot, and it worked perfectly every time. We ended up doing seven takes, two of which we had to drop in the middle for reasons I can't remember, but the other five were "keepers," as they say. I'm not sure which take we used, but the entire scenario is a single shot lasting around five and a half minutes. I'm pleased we were able to shoot it as a single continuous wide view from beginning to end because I believe it's what makes the action so compelling. I still make frittatas all the time, but no matter what pan I use, they always stick, and I despise myself for not packing the perfect pan in my suitcase on the last day of filming.

Here's a frittata recipe that Gianni Scappin taught me.

Chapter 7.

THE ANDOUILLETTE OFFENSIVE

Eating given meals on film sets can be a terrifying experience. The general rule is that the higher the budget, the finer the cuisine. Union laws govern when and how long a lunch break is taken on any specific film, and these restrictions differ by nation. However, rather than taking a lunch break, as an actor and director, I prefer to shoot "continuous days," also known as "French hours." This is sometimes referred to as a "running lunch," because tiny plates of food or sandwiches are always available throughout the day, and a brief break is taken about halfway through the day for cast and crew to grab a quick bite or a little rest. I've always found that doing so not only shortens the shooting day, but also increases efficiency. French hours are extremely popular in England and Europe, but not so much in the United States, for reasons I've never understood. I know I'm not writing a book about the workings of the film industry, which would be even more tedious than this memoir, but it's important to understand that food on set not only feeds people, but it also influences the budget, the structure of a shooting day, and how well a cast and crew work together.

Now, before you fall asleep, here's a look at how catering works in most movies. A cooked lunch will be offered when an actor arrives on site in the morning, which can typically be between 4:30 and 7:00 a.m., depending on the complexity of the makeup, costume, or scene to be shot that day. The assistant directors, runners, wardrobe, and hair and makeup artists are the first people to arrive on set. When the actor arrives, they will have either eaten or be in the process of eating breakfast. Breakfast will be served on tables under a gigantic marquee in a high-budget film. There will be steam trays of pre-fried eggs, scrambled eggs, bacon, hash browns, platters of smoked salmon, fruit, industrial toasters for toasting bagels, white bread, butter, jam, honey, yogurt, fruit juices, and coffee and tea urns. If the money is sufficient and the producer loves their employees and their hard work, an omelette station and other amenities will be provided. These are the types of producers who always engage a fantastic craft service caterer to provide a table of savory and sweet delights, as well as a truck selling miniature sandwiches, smoothies, cappuccinos, and so on, to keep guests content for potentially fifteen-hour days. Again, this applies primarily to films with exceptionally large budgets. Most films use a single truck with a few struggling caterers trying their best with little resources to keep a cast and crew fed and slightly satisfied. Every day, the caterers are the first to come at some obscene hour, and they begin cooking two dinners for at least fifty people. The ingredients are not always of the highest quality, and their resources (and, unfortunately, talents) are frequently stretched to the limit in order to offer a variety of dishes every day for what could be an eight-week shoot.

To accommodate so many people, each lunch includes a beef or chicken dish, a fish dish, two starches, two vegetables, a vegetarian dish, a salad or two, and dessert. Even with a large budget, this is not an easy assignment, and I do not envy their situation. Unfortunately, most caterers aren't up to the task, so many clients have stopped eating before the end of the movie. Certain cast and crew members will bring their own food if they have time to shop and prepare it, which will be challenging considering the long and erratic working hours. When an actor arrives on set, they normally place their breakfast order with the second assistant director (who oversees the base camp where all of the trailers are put up) before being led to hair and makeup. An actor has eaten breakfast while a subpar makeup artist tries to paint foundation on a masticating jaw and bobbing Adam's apple while politely ignoring the sulphurous odor of the actor's hard-boiled eggs. It's also in the makeup trailer, which serves as a safe haven for actors to ensure they get the best cup of coffee on location because most makeup professionals have nice coffee machines. However, just in case, I always bring at least two Nespresso machines with me on the first day of a job: one for the cosmetics trailer, which serves as a community supply of caffeine, and one for my own trailer, where I am frequently confined for hours on end and require a strong coffee when I need one.

Robert Altman was a fantastic film director and producer who made a number of excellent and significant films during his fifty-year career, including M*A*S*H, Nashville, and Gosford Park. Bob had produced an Alan Rudolph film that Campbell Scott and a few of my pals were working on in Montreal. Campbell and I had agreed to co-direct Big Night and would meet on a monthly basis to plan how we would shoot the film if we ever got the money. Campbell recommended I go to the set while he was filming Alan's movie because he thought I'd like the way it was filmed. Kate and I spent the weekend there, visiting friends and seeing the process. Alan asked me to return in a few weeks for a little job, which I gladly accepted. Following that, Campbell and I approached Altman to see if he would produce our film and lead us through the tough process of obtaining funding. We anticipated that having someone with his reputation and experience would help two first-time directors get inside Hollywood's closed doors. He agreed to assist that foot after reading the script and visiting with us. Despite his tight schedule, Bob was quite generous with his time, and when I told him I'd like to witness him on set, he was delighted to oblige. Soon after, I flew to Paris for a week to see Bob operate Prêt-a-Porter. The film's cast included a who's who of major, independent, and foreign film stars, some of whom I knew. It was incredible for me to see Bob in his usual casual but distinctive manner and to meet some of my favorite actors, like Sophia Loren and Marcello Mastroianni. When the two stars were filming a scene one day, they wanted to tell Altman something but couldn't due of the language barrier. Because I spoke a little Italian, I served as a translator, and the problem was solved by hook or crook. Mastroianni approached me after filming that day and invited me to join him and producer Jon Kilik for dinner. Marcello Mastroianni was and remains one of my all-time acting inspirations. Aside from being extremely beautiful and debonair, his performances ranged from deeply moving to mildly amusing. Even the birth of my children has not given me the same pleasure as that offer. Okay, the youngsters were the first to enter the planet, but only by a whisker. Literally. Anyway, when Mr. Mastroianni scrawled the restaurant's name on a ripped piece of paper in a shaky cigarette-stained hand and handed it to me, I guess I bowed like a geisha in gratitude.

It was an honor and a pleasure to work on Nora Ephron's Julie & Julia, playing Julia Child's husband, Paul, alongside Meryl Streep's Julia. As previously stated, I was a fan of Julia Child from an early age and was excited to explore the world Nora had so meticulously crafted. A lot of research is required for many tasks, but it isn't always as enjoyable as it was this time. In this case, I read everything I could about Julia and Paul, spent time with Paul's great-nephew, the wonderful writer Alex Prud'homme, and cooked a variety of recipes from Julia's Mastering the Art of French Cooking, which my mother had given me years ago, to get a true taste of his life. (In fact, Meryl and I cooked blanquette de veau for Kate and our friend Wren Arthur one night, which surprisingly turned out fairly good, although we served supper two hours later than anticipated due to disarray and inadequate preparation; I blame the film's star.)

Paul Child was an intriguing person. He was a judo expert, painter, and photographer (despite having only one eye due to a childhood accident), spoke fluent French, worked in the OSS (the precursor to the CIA) in Sri Lanka, where he met Julia, and eventually joined the American diplomatic corps after WWII, serving as a cultural liaison in France, Germany, and Norway. He was an avid reader and eater, thus he was knowledgeable about a wide range of topics. Paul encouraged Julia to study cooking during their time abroad, and she later applied her skills to television when they returned to the United States in the early 1960s. He was retired at the time and assisted her behind the scenes by moving her kitchen set from studio to studio, assisting with prep work, washing pots and pans at the end of the day, and drawing and shooting her cookbooks. In a nutshell, he was a fairly accomplished man for his time and one of the most fascinating persons I've ever performed with. Nora, Meryl, and the joyful environment on site greatly enhanced the overall experience. As I may have said on other pages, this is a very rare occurrence.

That attitude lasted when we reconvened for our press tour a year later. To begin, when President and Mrs. Obama were first elected, they chose Julie & Julia as the first film to be shown in the White House screening room, an event to which we were all happy to be invited. When we arrived, the president and First Lady greeted us and were so nice that we struggled not to swoon. After a brief talk, President Obama departed to attend to state business, leaving Mrs. Obama and the rest of us to see the film in the small White House screening room. We understood that no matter where we went on the rest of the press trip, we'd have a hard time following in his footsteps. However, there was one more experience that stood out for quite different reasons. I don't remember the name of a modest café just inland from the Normandy coast, which is probably a good thing. Meryl, Chris

Messina, and I ended up here one afternoon while traveling from Deauville to Paris. We were promoting Julie & Julia at the Deauville film festival, which is one of my favorites because it is far more relaxed than most other large festivals. There is a good amount of tedious press interviews to be done in Deauville, as well as a few photo sessions (always unpleasant), but screenings are only held during the day, leaving the evenings and nights free. Guests will stay at the Hotel Barrière Le Royal, which overlooks the seemingly endless beaches immortalized by the painter Boudin more than a century ago. The air is crisp, and the skies are blue until they suddenly darken and unleash a massive thunderstorm, making the entire experience quite romantic. The festival and its surrounds are a filmmaker and filmgoer's paradise. The environment is a foodie's paradise.

That stretch of the Gallic coast is notable for both seafood and more rustic country fare. The poolside buffet lunch at the Hotel Le Royal is a classic Norman experience in and of itself. Platters of fruits de mer on ice, crisp green salads with a classic shallot dressing, fresh baguettes, and bottles of rosé or Sancerre are available and quickly consumed by all guests. If you wish to venture out of the Barrière bubble, there are several excellent eateries in the vicinity. I'd been to the festival numerous times previously, staying for varying lengths of time, but this time I was only there for a few days because we had a film premiere and a press junket in Paris. On the morning of our departure, we followed a procession of cars going north to our destination, stopping briefly at the D-Day beaches. As a WWII buff, I was overjoyed to visit this area that I'd read so much about. Needless to say, it was more fascinating and moving than I could have anticipated, and I am still amazed by the experience years later. We rejoined our convoy and stopped for lunch at a little country cafe that one of the drivers knew about. As usual, we arrived to a little cafe down a side road, hungry and thirsty for grapes. M. The cast of characters around the table included Streep, my PR Jenn, Chris Messina, Meryl's brother Dana, who is an avid eater, and me. The proprietor, who was probably not as happy to greet Meryl as our D-Day beach tour guide, noticed our presence and promptly handed us bread, water, the menu, and, thankfully, wine.

We were starving, but we also knew we were going to Paris, where we would eat a lot of excellent food, so we all promised to be careful with our lunch orders. The cuisine was largely regional, with an emphasis on meat and game rather than fish. Appetizers included eggs mayonnaise and mâche salad, as well as entrées including onglet, omelette aux herbes, and tripes à Caen. While scanning the menu, I discovered that andouillette was a house specialty. I thought it looked interesting and asked Meryl if she had ever eaten it. She claimed she hadn't, but because we both liked andouille sausages, we assumed it had to be a smaller version because the name ended in "ette." When the pleasant owner and waitress returned, we ordered our appetizers (along with extra wine, which had obviously evaporated in the afternoon heat) and inquired about the andouillette. They clarified that it was a sausage, to which we replied that of course we understood (without overstating our knowledge) and that it was peculiar to Normandy. With the exception of Jenn, we all ordered the andouillette with excitement, followed by a kind of "Bring it on!" sweeping wave of the arm, as if the "ugly American" is an endangered species. Our host took note of our order and kindly left. The waitress arrived shortly later with our drinks. As our corks popped, we discussed the festival and how fortunate we had been to get a private tour of the D-Day memorial site, or at least to follow Meryl's private tour. Our appetizers arrived, and we ummed and ahhed while ordering additional wine since... There was none left in the bottles, so I presume we completed it. We ate fast while the server replenished our glasses, and before we knew it, we had finished our first course. Our entrees arrived after a brief pause. Jenn's vivid green salad was presented to her, but the rest of us were served a meal like a horse cock. Meryl's expression slumped substantially, and she let out a little "Oh."

She bit off a portion and put it in her mouth. She chewed slowly. In a brief second, her face reflected a lifetime of human emotion. She took a swallow. She placed a napkin against her lips. She spoke in quiet tone.

MERYL: It does have a barnyard feel to it.

I put a morsel into my mouth and, before it had passed my second taste bud, I was vomiting it into my plate, attempting not to projectile-vomit the culmination of two gluttonous days all over my colleagues. I spilled my wine, ate half a baguette, and then had more wine. Dana had tucked into the item thoroughly and appeared to be doing fine until he was halfway through his second forkful, when he turned to face me, his eyes wide with fear. Grabbing his napkin, he wiped the crumbs away and shouted, "EErgaarhhuergh! Christ!"

Chris Messina returned to the table, staring at his awaiting entrée. As he took his seat, we all cried, "ALL THREE! Don't touch that!"

CHRIS: Why is that? Is it all three? Simply do not. Don't.

When the waitress inquired whether everything was fine, we assured her that it was. I even complimented the dish, but as she walked away, I noticed a slight smirk on her lips. The owner returned a few moments later, perplexed.

Andouillette is the owner. It's not...

ALL FOUR OF US: It's great, but not what we expected. It's nothing like the ones we've had...

He smiled and nodded understandingly as more sad justifications and lies were spoken. After a few moments, he motioned for the waitress, who had been amusingly hovering behind him, to empty our plates and asked if we wanted anything else.

ALL FOUR OF US: Please have four omelettes.

OWNER: Is this all there is to it?

AND MORE WINE FOR THE FOUR OF US.

As we waited for our seemingly harmless entrées, we realized that it wasn't simply the courageous Allied forces who had forced the Germans to retreat. The Nazi retreat was most likely motivated by the prospect of having to eat andouillette every day as penance for their violent takeover of Normandy.

This is an objective, politically correct definition of andouillette from Wikipedia.

Andouillette is a coarse-grained sausage made from pork (or sometimes veal), chitterlings (intestine), pepper, wine, onions, and seasonings. Tripe, or cow stomach lining, is occasionally used as a filler in andouillette, but it is not the casing or the essential ingredient in its creation. True andouillette will look like an oblong tube. When formed using the small intestine, it is a fat sausage of 25 mm in diameter; but, when made with the colon, it is much larger, possibly 7-10 cm in diameter, and has a stronger aroma. True andouillette is rare outside of France and has a strong, distinct odor due to its digestive origins and ingredients. Although it may appear disgusting to the ignorant, this aspect of andouillette is widely treasured by its fans.

Do I need to say anything else?

Chapter 8.

THE WEDDING FEAST

Felicity Blunt, my wife, and I met at her sister's wedding a little over a year after Kate's death. The wedding took place in Lake Como on a gorgeous villa owned by a couple's friend whose name rhymes with George Clooney. I'd boarded the train from Florence to visit my parents, three children, a stepdaughter, and father-in-law in Tuscany. Kate and I had always intended to take this tour with all of the above, but we were never able to due to her long illness, so I decided to do it in her honor.

The wedding lasted three days, and since I hadn't been away from my family in a long time prior to Kate's death, it was a wonderful and, as I discovered, much-needed vacation. I saw some old acquaintances and made some new ones, including my friend's sister, whom I would marry a few years later. Felicity and I chatted a lot during those several days, which meant she was practically stalking me. (There is surveillance footage.) The majority of our chat was on food. Conveniently, I was about to begin filming Captain America in London, where she lived, and we decided to meet for dinner. As a result, a food-focused connection developed.

During our short weeks in London, we ate at a number of wonderful restaurants, the first of which was the recently closed Ledbury, run by two-Michelin-starred chef Brett Graham and conveniently located above Felicity's apartment.

Now, I am not really drawn to the Michelin star. Many of the restaurants that have gotten this prestigious award are, to say the least, choosy, and I've left a few of them completely hungry, as I've never found pretentiousness to be particularly filling. The Ledbury, however, was not.

The little dining room was lovely; the tables were spaced apart, and even when it was full, it appeared like there were more workers than diners. The warmth that both the room and the people exuded immediately put you at ease. I attribute this to Brett's demeanor, because, as they say, "the fish stinks from the head down," yet it was a lovely odor. Brett was not impressed by the delicious supper at the Ledbury. He is surprisingly pleasant and calm for someone who works so hard and maintains such a high standard of excellence for so long. (The Ledbury has long been recognized as one of the world's top fifty restaurants.)

Felicity suggested we get the tasting menu the first time we ate at the Ledbury so we could try as many of Brett's culinary and wine pairings as possible. Every item, from the Kumamoto oysters to the stuffed rabbit loin, was superb. During our following visits, we almost invariably ordered the tasting menu. Brett was kind enough to take us inside the kitchen for a tour one night after another delicious dinner.

The kitchen was modest and unattractive in relation to the exceptional quality and complexity of the meals provided on a nightly basis. After a few minutes of looking around, we both noticed two pheasants, mostly dead but still complete with feathers, sitting on a tray on the countertop. We started oohing and ahhing over them and were about to ask Brett how he might prepare them when he asked if we wanted to take them home. Because my wife is an agent and I am an actor, we both know a good deal when we see one, so after Brett explained how to "cold pluck" them, we hurried the fowl, tray and all, upstairs to her apartment and refrigerated them overnight.

The next morning, a Saturday, we awoke with the excitement that comes from knowing you have a passionate goal to pursue. We got the pheasants out of the fridge, made a morning beverage, and sat in front of the television to watch Saturday Kitchen, my new favorite show, while plucking our birds. An hour and a half later, our dressing robes were covered in feathers, and the tray contained the avian gifts Brett had bestowed on us the night before. It had been a wonderful morning. Two food nerds become closer emotionally by ripping the feathers from two deceased birds. It defies logic that this could offer us both so much joy, yet it did. To begin with, if you're a foodie, there's always something fulfilling about getting to know the vegetable, fruit, or animal before it becomes your food, whether you grew it, raised it, or hunted it. Making that connection and then connecting with someone else at the same time is a higher, even spiritual level of gastronomical intimacy. It was one of the most romantic mornings I'd ever spent seated. I'm not sure how we prepared the pheasant, but that doesn't matter in this case. Sometimes the process is more delightful than the result.

Felicity and I would always go there for special occasions until the Ledbury's untimely and very terrible closure, and even though Brett was constantly adding new dishes, if it was on the menu, we'd always get the pheasant as a nice memento of when we first plucked together.

The second restaurant we visited was the now-defunct L'Anima, led by chef Francesco Mazzei. (I am starting to wonder whether Felicity and I are cursed.) Francesco, like my family, is from Calabria, yet his cuisine is not restricted to regional specialties. Francesco is one of those chefs who can adapt classic dishes without overcomplicating the method or jeopardizing the dish's integrity. Felicity and I ate there for three hours the first time we visited. We were served course after course of exquisite food, all washed down with excessive amounts of wine. I finally had to stop eating, not just because my jet lag was setting in, but also because I was about to pass out.

Felicity, precious and slender. Felicity, on the other hand, was unwilling to give up. She finished her final course, as well as the rest of mine, and continued to talk as if it wasn't past midnight and she didn't have to be at work the next morning. She then observed a cheese cart rolling into the dining room from the corner of her still-hungry eye.

"A cheese cart!" Yummy! Let's start with cheese, shall we? "Do you want some cheese?"

"Well, I mean... sure, if you—"

Please pardon me! Could we take a look at the—???!!!"

She had caught the waiter's attention with the wheels on wheels and successfully intercepted him, despite the fact that I am confident he was on his way to another table. (When she wants something, she has an incredible capacity to demand attention that only the British possess. Is it due of their accent? She is not a snob, but her education, as well as her innate intelligence and warmth, are readily apparent when she speaks. I think the combination of all of these attributes explains why she is so successful, has so many wonderful friends, and I never win an argument. So, before I knew it, the cheese cart was in front of us, and she began grilling the server about the lactic content, provenance, and flavor character of each cheese. She then requested additional slabs, which she devoured as if she hadn't eaten in days, along with some dessert wine from the chef. What happened after that is a blur, but we were seriously dating before I knew it, and avoiding gout became part of my daily routine.

Whenever I visited Felicity in London, whether with or without my children, we always made a point of going to L'Anima. Francesco became more generous with each visit, frequently denying payment outright, particularly when the children were present. We were so impressed by his dishes and the space's minimalist, contemporary design that we decided to hold our wedding celebration there a few years later. Of course, we had a series of tastings to choose the canapés and other meals. (Oliver, my father-in-law, participated in one of these gustatory marathons and still talks about it.) After a few of these ancient-Rome-style feasts, we decided on a menu that could serve 156 people. Following the three-course meal, participants were free to mingle and leisurely stroll over tables stacked high with various dolci, freely pouring from bottles of every digestif available in the UK. Francesco suggested that if there were enough wine-soaked stragglers left partying after midnight, he could serve "una spaghettata!," which is simply a shitload of spaghetti with a plain tomato sauce. We both agreed. The wedding day was a resounding success because to Felicity's meticulous planning, L'Anima's great crew, and Francesco's culinary skills.

As previously indicated, we offered some dolci in the form of pastries and such, but you may have noticed that I did not mention a cake, as in a traditional tiered frosted confection. This is understandable given that neither Felicity nor I have a sweet craving, but we did provide a savory option. This was a massive six-story structure made entirely of... wheels of cheese. "So, what's that you're doing right now?"

"I'm fluffing them up."

"Oh," I replied, my uncertainty increasing.

I moved away to get a glass of wine, and when I returned, Felicity had completed the fluffing process by opening the oven door, letting out a plume of greasy smoke, and removing the roasting pan of simmering goose fat. "My father and I tried not to panic as the room filled with smoke and Felicity carefully placed the pan of scorching liquid bird flab on the stovetop." Sorry. As we rushed to open the windows and turn off the fire alarm, she giggled, sounding more British than ever.

"What the hell are you doing?" I eventually enquired.

"I'm making roast potatoes!"

"Like that?"

"Yes!" she said, her voice growing furious.

"But, what's all the oil?" I asked, trying not to panic.

"That's goose fat." And this is where they are cooked! Just unwind."

My father was standing by the open door to the garden, fanning away the smoke with a tea towel, while my mother stood at the kitchen doorway, brow wrinkled, safely away from the churning pan of fat. Felicity then took the potatoes one at a time, carefully placing them in the pan, and neatly pushing the entire thing back into the oven. For a brief while, there was silence.

"When you said roasted potatoes, I thought that you meant—"

"You thought I meant the way you make them," she said, laughing.

"Yes. Just chop them up and add some garlic—"

My mother, who had crept back into the room, spoke out. "Yes, with garlic, olive oil, rosemary, and salt, and then just... you know... roasted."

Felicity chuckled and smiled. "Those, yes." I enjoy them, but this is how we do it. Roast potatoes from England. They are served alongside a Sunday roast. This includes Yorkshire puddings. "My grandmother taught my mother and me."

"That's how much oil they used?" I inquired skeptically.

"Goose fat."

"Sorry, goose fat."

"You can use oil if you like—"

"What kind?" my now-inquisitive mother asked, having slipped back into the room, figuring the situation was clear.

"Vegetable. But goose fat is the best. It merely increases the flavor. "And to answer your question, dear," she said emphatically, "this is the amount of oil they used." I guarantee they will be fantastic.

"Well, I hope so, because you almost burned the house down," I remarked with a smile.

There was a brief period of silence. Felicity focused her gaze on me. My parents felt the same way. The two people who brought me into this world quickly supported my girlfriend and turned against me, saying things like, "She knows what she's doing!" It's okay! It is just a cloud of smoke! "Leave her alone..." and so on.

The oven erupted again at that point. When my parents observed the fatty vapours, they quickly retreated to the open doorways for protection, but they continued to wield cudgels on Felicity's behalf.

"Whoops!" Felicity said, grabbing a mitt and fork. She removed the pan from the oven, delicately flipped the potatoes with a fork, slid them back in, and closed the door.

"There we are!" she shouted, clutching more greasy puffs. "Not much longer now!"

I was madly in love. My parents were as well. Then we ate her potatoes and fell in love again.

Chapter 9.

COMMUNITY TIES

Felicity suggested organizing a party during one of her first trips to us in Westchester prior to our wedding. She even suggested having a feast and preparing a suckling pig. I immediately agreed because I and the kids both like suckling pigs. Felicity and I called the butcher in the next town about acquiring the piglet, and he assured us that he'd be able to get one before the weekend. But I must take a time to discuss something that is fading—and it is not one of my disks.

Butcher shops and fishmongers were common when I was younger, and certainly before I was born, until massive supermarkets invaded the suburbs and, unfortunately, our cities, leaving them obsolete. Those that remain are usually rather pleasant, but their menus are not particularly experimental, and their prices are excessive. This, however, is one of my favorite elements of life in England. Although I am aware that individually owned butcher shops and fishmongers are diminishing in the UK, there are still a significant number of them when compared to the US. I am quite lucky to have both, both of which are of very high quality, within walking distance of my house, and I visit one or the other every few days. Even when I'm out running errands or between appointments in various districts of London, I can't help but stop in at every butcher shop or fishmonger I see. I visit them in the same way I would an art gallery. I'm not there to buy anything; I just want to watch the spectacle. I love that many butchers in London still wear banded straw hats like in the old days, and that, in addition to the standard cuts of meat and sausages, various kinds of offal are available, which I rarely see in the States. Many people are afraid by bleeding platters containing dismembered animal parts, but I am fascinated by them and the many ways they can be transformed into something magnificent.

Most people are turned off by the aromas emanating from a fish market or a fishmonger's, and they will cover their noses as they pass by. But after taking a deep breath, I can't help but want to enter, or at least gaze through the window. I enjoy the crisp saline aroma emanating from a vibrant array of fresh fish. I appreciate how they're proudly displayed in the exhibits and refrigerated cases, with the shine and shimmer of their scales highlighted by the brilliant lights above and crushed ice crystals below. I appreciate seeing fishmongers painstakingly scale and debone a fish while speaking with a customer about how fresh it is, explaining that severe weather is causing a lack of a particular catch, or perhaps recommending a method for preparing the sea creature in hand to a customer who is frightened of fish.

It still amazes me how many people refuse to eat or cook fish out of fear. This is where the fishmonger comes in useful. Not only will you get a premium product from someone who knows where it came from, whether it's sustainable, when it arrived, and how long it will last in the fridge (all of which I know can be found written on packaged fish these days), but the fishmonger will also be able to teach you how to cook it, even in the most basic of ways. This interaction between buyer and seller deepens our attachment to the item we are purchasing. Eating healthy, to me, is about building relationships through food, not just about what tastes good. I'm not saying anything new when I say that our relationships to what we eat have mostly evaporated beneath layers of plastic wrap. The incredible, critical human connections we may have when we purchase something we enjoy eating from someone who enjoys selling it, who obtained it from someone who enjoys growing, capturing, or raising it are also dwindling. Whether we recognize it or not, these links bring us great comfort and are a crucial part of what makes a community strong.

Ray Oldenburg authored a beautiful novel titled The Great Good Place. In it, he addresses how we have two significant domains in our lives: home and work. However, what he refers to as the third place is as vital since it allows us to perform better in the first two. Pubs, cafés, and restaurants are examples of "third places". They bring people from all walks of life together and allow us to interact casually with people we don't work with or know. As we all know, especially in the aftermath of a global epidemic, this bond is essential for both the individual and society as a whole in order to function and thrive. For the reasons described above, I would say that independent shops, particularly food shops, also serve this purpose, and their demise to a flood of chain stores is a tragedy for all of us.

When I stroll into my local fish market, I am greeted pleasantly, asked about my children, chit-chatted about the weather, and told what catch they personally think is "lovely" on any given day. They then inquire about the dish I am making. When I say I'm going to make a seafood stew, the first question is, "For how many?" and we're off to choose any combination of cod, hake, haddock, clams, mussels, prawns, langoustines, and scallops for the stew, oysters for an appetizer, and samphire because I have to buy it if it's available in their chilly displays. I As we select each component, we consider whether its size or count is appropriate for the number of visitors. When everything is measured, wrapped, and bagged, the fishmonger will always add a whole lemon or two, a few sprigs of curly parsley, and a small jar of their homemade frozen fish stock to the bag. Yes, it was pricey, but it was well worthwhile. We say our goodbyes, knowing that in the coming days, we'll wave to each other as I walk by their shop and quickly calculate how much of each fish, crustacean, or mollusk will be necessary when I'm lucky enough to bless my table with their aquatic gems again.

However, I was writing about pigs.

So Felicity and I drove to a butcher shop in nearby Ridgefield, Connecticut, on a Friday afternoon, bought a suckling pig weighing about twenty pounds, and took it home. We intended to roast it on the rotisserie on the outdoor grill because it was too enormous to fit in our ovens; however, the pig proved too long for even the rotisserie. I did have a wood-burning pizza oven that would be suitable, but having never cooked a suckling pig before and being concerned about my inability to keep the oven at a consistent temperature, I concluded that it would almost surely end in disaster. We just had one option: decapitation. To carry out the act, I grabbed a large carbon steel knife and a cleaver, both of which belonged to my paternal grandfather. He'd used them to skin and break down animals he'd shot during hunting trips to Vermont, where he owned acreage. So, channeling the real Stanley Tucci, I sliced the flesh away from the neck with the knife and delivered the cleaver's cutting final strokes, decreasing the length of our porcine purchase. We then impaled it on the spit and transferred it to the grill, where it just fit. The school bus arrived at the end of the drive at the same moment, and they came a-running across the grass, full of the exuberant energy that all children have on Friday afternoons.

"Hey, guys, come and see what we got!" I yelled.

"Is it the PIG??!!!" they shouted.

"Yes!"

They ran up the patio stairs, flung their backpacks on the ground, and looked at the pig with curiosity.

"Where's the head?" they asked.

"We had to cut it off because it didn't fit on the barbecue."

"Awwwww," they cried. "Why didn't you wait for us!?"

Felicity and I exchanged glances.

"Sorry," I apologized. "I didn't think—" "We'll get another pig someday, and then you can watch us cut its head off," Felicity sweetly vowed, sounding like a Hollywood serial killer.

They weren't convinced.

"Where is it?" they asked.

"Right here," I said, taking it off the counter for them to check.

"Wow!"

They began poking and prodding it with their tiny fingers, scrutinizing its lips and eyes like agitated, clumsy veterinarians.

"What're you gonna do with it?"

"Well, I was actually going to just try slow-roasting it in the pizza oven."

"Oh, okay, yes. "Wow...," they exclaimed, as if going to devour it, but I knew they weren't. The tender, juicy white meat of the carcass and the crunch of the cracklings were all they desired.

We shooed them inside to wash their hands and cooked the antithesis of slow-roasted pig's head, Ritz crackers coated with peanut butter, after they spent a little more time looking at the head and making preadolescent comments about how the rotisserie spit gets rammed unkindly up the pig's rectum. The following day, we cooked the pig as planned, but it was too heavy for the rotisserie, which broke halfway through. Every few minutes, my friend Oliver Platt, a superb gourmet, and I took turns spinning the device manually. Needless to say, neither the pig nor my attempt to slow-roast the skull were successful. I was so focused in supervising the carcass that I completely forgot about the head, only realising it later that afternoon. When I opened the pizza oven, I was faced with a scene from a horror film, which I will not describe here. To summarize, I loathe horror films.

The second time we attempted to roast a whole pig—the pig redux—we were lucky to have an expert on hand to assist us: Adam Perry Lang. Adam is an excellent chef and restaurateur who can prepare almost anything, but his main love and talent is meat. He co-owned a restaurant in London called Barbecoa with Jamie Oliver, which was next to a butcher shop that served some of the best beef, fowl, and game in town. (Unfortunately, both are no longer operational.) Adam left London seven years ago to relocate to the United States, where he now co-owns APL with his buddy, foodie, and all-around great person Jimmy Kimmel. These two guys and their wives were the ones to send Felicity and me a Caja China as an engagement gift. I had no idea what a Caja China was, but when I saw one, I knew I'd seen one before.

A Caja China is essentially a rectangular metal box on wheels, with an aluminum and plywood frame. The box is large enough to house a side of beef, a significant number of ribs, or nearly twenty fowl. Most notably, there's a huge pig. Adam and his then-wife, Fleur, were visiting family in New York and decided to spend the weekend here.

He explained that they intended to use the Caja China to roast a whole pig. He handed us a shopping list and promised to get the pig for us. When Felicity and I hear the term "pig," we think of "party." As a result, we threw one.

Adam and Fleur arrived the day before the celebration, followed by the pig, weighing seventy pounds. Adam and I took it to the patio and arranged it on a picnic table covered in plastic tablecloths. He carefully removed the tenderloins from the carcass, as they are too fragile and thin to be cooked in this manner, and left them aside before we went inside to make the brine.

Chapter 10.

COOKING, CLEANING, CRYING

The sense of freedom that cruising the Amalfi coast afforded contrasts sharply with the restricted lifestyle that March 2020, also known as the first lockdown, placed on all of us. (We hoped this was the only lockdown.) During that time, I wrote this piece. It describes a day in our lives and the events that occur on that day, which effectively repeat themselves for months. We were in London with my wife, Felicity, and our two little children, a boy, five, and a girl, two; my three older children, a girl, eighteen, and boy/girl twins, twenty; and a university girlfriend who couldn't see her parents overseas. Cramming all of these people with different personalities, ages, needs, and desires into a house for six weeks resulted in a unique dynamic. For the most part, everything went smoothly, therefore no one was murdered. Initially, I had high hopes for how we could pass the time in a convivial and enjoyable manner. I pictured a rotating cast of cooks for the evening meal, followed by movies, games, or Bordeaux-fueled charades around the fire. Things didn't go exactly as anticipated. Instead, here is how our typical lockdown day went without our nanny and weekly cleaning person.

7:00 A.M. GMT

Within moments of Felicity and I waking up, our five-year-old had entered our room. It's unclear how he knows we're awake. He could be wearing a device identical to the one we use to monitor his two-year-old sister. He moves over to my wife's side of the bed, completely ignoring me, and begins talking to her about anything and everything. (He frequently discusses dragons because he is obsessed with the fantastic book series How to Train Your Dragon and its several cinematic adaptations.) Felicity and I head to the bathroom, and he follows us there, perching himself on the bidet to regale us with innovative plot points and insights into the seemingly infinite variety of dragons and their distinguishing features. He'll keep going like this till the sun sets. We head to his sister's room after dressing, where she has been "singing" in her cot and reading the shredded remains of her massive Peppa Pig book collection. When she notices us, she covers her face behind a book and pretends to be asleep. She finds it humorous. She is right. I change her "nappy" and she kicks me in the groin numerous times for my trouble. We all head downstairs to eat breakfast. I'll have a double espresso, orange juice, and a bowl of cereal with banana and almond milk. I also take D3, K2, C, B12, curcumin powder, and joint supplements to protect my knees from splitting like a melting glacier whenever I bend down to pick up a loose Lego brick. Felicity drinks tea, while the children have toast, cereal, fruit, the occasional egg, or whatever their tiny hearts desire. The majority of their meals wind up on the floor. This leads to my first full cleaning of the day.

8:00 A.M. GMT

I clean up their mess, empty the dishwashers (yes, we have two), scrub the counters, wipe down the cabinets and their handles, and organize the refrigerator contents, discarding anything over the expiration date. I sweep the floor as well, but after exercising considerable restraint, I decide to postpone mopping until after lunch.

As you might have guessed, I am a neat freak. I adore cleaning because it helps me relax. However, I went above and beyond during the lockdown. I got a notion the other day that I could strap a vacuum to my back like a leaf blower and have it with me at all times. This is not a positive indicator.

8:45 a.m. GMT.

Felicity and I did an online workout with a Pilates instructor friend of ours. We asked one of the older children to come down and babysit this morning the night before. The bleary-eyed applicant comes seconds before the class begins, face puffy from sleep, and groans a "Good morning" as we rush to the living room for a workout-filled vacation from reality. During this time, I consider what we could cook for eight people that evening.

9:45 a.m. GMT.

After the lesson, Felicity and I talk about which food items need to be replenished. The amount of food, beer, and wine consumed by four people aged eighteen to twenty is staggering. If there are no avocados in the stores, it is because we have consumed them all. If there is no Kerrygold butter left in the UK, it is either frozen or eaten. It is all there. I actually ate it. Most certainly, without spreading it on anything. When I noticed a neighbour staring at our cat the other day, I realized she hadn't eaten meat in a week since my gluttonous family had consumed all of the beef, lamb, veal, chicken, oxtail, hog, rabbit, and game in southwest London. I rummage in the fridge, still gasping for air after a very difficult workout.

Given our limited supplies, I decided on a simple dinner of pasta alla Norma and sautéed lamb chops. I feel that these two dishes will satisfy everyone's taste and nutritional needs, though I know that my eighteen-year-old daughter, who is now vegetarian, will only eat the spaghetti meal. What a coincidence.

10:30 a.m. GMT.

Felicity goes upstairs to shower and start her remote workday from our bedroom after finishing some homeschooling with the five-year-old. She works as a literary agent and conducts all of her meetings through Zoom. With the exception of doing voiceover work for a CNN series that I recently did remotely from my studio, I don't have much to do these days because film and television production has stopped. As far as I know, this has never happened since someone first yelled "Action!" more than a century ago.

So I wash laundry and play with the kids, frequently inventing games like "Mean King," in which I pretend to have a highly aristocratic

British accent and they come to me to "pay their taxes," only to "steal" them back when I "take a nap." This game appeals to me because it allows me to sit on my "throne," an Eero Saarinen womb chair, which is the most comfortable seating device ever designed. I attempt to keep the game going as long as possible so I don't have to get up, but when the two-year-old starts reeking, I realize I've neglected my diaper-changing duty. When the wrestling match is finished and she has accused everyone else in the house of pooping except herself, I change the kids out of their jammies and into their daytime clothes. Although the five-year-old cannot clothe himself, he admits now that he is unable to do so. As a result, I guide him through each stage as the two-year-old runs around laughing and jeering at me. I eventually catch her, throw her against the sofa, and force her into the first of many costumes for the day, like sausage meat into a casing. My glasses are missing, so I can't see well enough to work the tiny buttons on children's clothing, so I leave a section of her costume undone, hoping Felicity will not notice. (No, she does not. But I do, and it disturbs me throughout the day.)

11:00 a.m. GMT.

When the kids are clothed, I take them outside to the garden, where they jump on the trampoline and beg me to let them play with the hose. I occasionally bounce or "wrestle" with them for a few moments, which they enjoy. It had the same impression on me. After a while, I gave in and allowed kids to play in the water with a hose, buckets, and a small plastic kitchen set. After the children have been sufficiently occupied, I walk inside and begin cooking while keeping an eye on them through the kitchen window. First, I opted to make chicken stock from the carcass.

12:15 p.m. GMT.

The older generation of children is gaining awareness. They enter the kitchen and quickly eat an entire loaf of bread, two pints of cherry tomatoes, four avocados, six eggs, two pints of blueberries, four bananas, twenty rashers of bacon, one litre of almond milk, six Nespresso pods, and a litre of orange juice before retreating to the TV room or their bedrooms, claiming to be doing their homework. Even if I disagree, I believe them. Felicity comes down to feed the kids lunch after I change their damp clothing. I'm going to clean a couple of bathrooms, do some laundry, or vacuum something I already vacuumed three hours ago.

1:45 p.m. GMT.

Felicity lays the two-year-old down to sleep, the five-year-old listens to his audiobook, and I prepare the marinara and eggplant for the pasta alla Norma.

3:00 pm GMT

When everything is prepared and the kitchen is clean, I intend to write, read, or catch up on emails. Instead, I do a crossword problem from the New York Times to clear my mind and easily fall asleep.

3:30 p.m. GMT.

I awoke with spittle on my chin and much too few questions addressed. I rush upstairs, checking my watch, to awaken the two-year-old from her slumber. When I arrive, Felicity is already on a conference call and changing herself. I understand she wants to give me a nasty look, but she is much more than that. I take the child, finish diapering her, and dress her before going downstairs. I offer both children a snack, and we play in the garden together. We jump on the trampoline, draw with chalk on the patio, look for slugs, and maybe paint. It is both delightful and draining. We're laughing one moment and crying the next, and I'm making decisions like, "Let her have it for a few minutes, then you can have it."

"What's a few?"

"A few is three."

"Three minutes?"

"Three minutes, yes." Then you might have it.

"Will you time it?"

"Yes, I will time it."

I time it, but the two-year-old screams when the item they both desire is taken away from her. The game restarts, but the spat resumes.

4:30 p.m. GMT.

I look at my watch and wish it was 5 o'clock. It's cocktail hour.

4:45 PM GMT

I give in and prepare a Negroni. Negronis are compared to breasts: "One is not enough, two is perfect, and three is just too many." I am tempted today to see what happens if I drink four.

5:00 PM GMT.

The older children have now returned downstairs to eat a full meal before I prepare them a complete meal for dinner. Fortunately, as penance, two of them take the children upstairs for a bath. Felicity enters the kitchen and asks a Negroni. I gladly make her one because I loathe drinking alone, though I do make allowances on a daily basis. In any case, drinking never really leaves you alone. Someone, somewhere, is constantly drinking. We prepare lamb chops, rice, and string beans for the children's lunch. I switch to white wine, and thank goodness it's evening.

6:00 PM GMT.

The children finish their meal, which sometimes requires coaxing, appealing, or threatening them with old chestnuts like, "There will be no dessert for you, young man," and "Do you think dragons leave food on their plates?".

"Dragons don't use plates."

"I understand that they don't use plates. I am only asking... Could you kindly finish it?

The kids are allowed to watch some television after lunch, sort of. He likes Peppa Pig, whereas she prefers Dragons. (There is no doubt that my wife and I, like many parents, wish the creators of that obnoxious cartoon swine a horrible death, but they are so wealthy that they have most likely bought immortality. At the same time, the aforementioned pig gives us a half-hour of relaxation each day. May God bless the creators.

While the kids are occupied, I begin preparing the meal for the next "sitting." We put the kids to bed once they've finished watching TV. The two-year-old is screaming between gulps of her bottle, as she always does when she is forced to leave her favorite pink porcine companion. We then take turns reading about dragons to the five-year-old, who then informs us that he is hungry, so we reluctantly prepare him some bread and say something like, "I told you to eat your dinner. "This is the last time."

That is it. Until next time.

7:45 p.m. GMT.

Felicity and I cook dinner for ourselves and the other four human locusts, eating standing around the kitchen island since we're too lazy to set the table. We eat, drink wine, and discuss food, but we haven't chatted much in the past week. This upsets me because I know we're all preoccupied with our own issues. I'm sure the twenty-year-olds are wondering if their year abroad will even materialize, and my eighteen-year-old is wondering how universities will select who gets accepted and who doesn't without any exams. Felicity is concerned about her assistant's trip, her parents' safety, and a variety of other issues.

I'm curious if my highly social parents are genuinely adopting social distancing, and I'm already thinking that I'll have to work on one of them for a while to make ends meet.

But, no matter how unhappy we are about the situation, I know we can't help but think about how lucky we are to have each other, a home over our heads, food in our stomachs, and no signs of illness. Only a few miles away, in any direction, are hospitals filled with sick and dying patients being cared for by overworked and overwhelmed National Health Service doctors, nurses, and support staff.

Because of the risk of infection, we can only write checks and earn money for charity and the NHS by producing home films. As we eat quietly, we all pray that this will end quickly and without further hardship, that our leaders will get at least one thing right along the way, and that the next time we are all trapped here, it will be by choice.

9:15 p.m. GMT.

After cleaning the kitchen together, we separated, the kids going to the TV room and my wife and I going to the sitting room to read. In a few minutes, I'll climb the stairs and stroll to bed, my knees moaning as I plan tomorrow night's food. Chicken cutlets for kids, mushroom risotto for adults.

The first lockdown began almost a year ago, and we are now nearly six weeks into the second. Obviously, the initial attempt failed. However, with few exceptions, it appears that people are taking things more seriously and adhering to the rules. Vaccines are being distributed, and the number of illnesses and deaths is rapidly decreasing, for which we are all grateful. During the first few weeks of this lockdown, all of the kids, including Isabel's boyfriend, were at home, thus a lot of food was purchased, cooked, and consumed, as previously reported. Nicolo, on the other hand, has returned to his flat and his "mates" (as he now refers to his friends) in Brighton to complete his online studies, while Isabel and her boyfriend have retreated to his house to retain their sanity. Camilla is the only one who remains with me, Felicity, Matteo, and Emilia. Despite this, Emilia is now speaking in complete words (albeit some are frequently incomprehensible) and conversing almost as much as her brother. Everyone had a nice time. (It is, actually.) Camilla bought a sewing machine to improve her mental health and frequently goes to her room to "thread her bobbins," as she puts it. But I can't help but think she's putting together a hot-air balloon to fly away from us all. I do not blame her. I did notice that several of our bed sheets were missing, as were all of our Fortnum & Mason hampers. Hmmm. Felicity and I, on the other hand, are just feeding five people this time. It is almost too straightforward. Almost.

Chapter 11.

COOKING IN THE DARK

Being in Los Angeles for more than a few days is unbearable for me. I've had that sensation about the site since my first visit, about 34 years ago. Although there are gorgeous locations, excellent restaurants, and close friends and family members I enjoy, it is simply not for me. I despise the perpetual sun, the lack of rain, the absence of seasons, and the overall sprawl. After a more than five-year hiatus, I returned four years ago to film the limited series Feud. I traveled back and forth from LA to London multiple times to avoid being away for too long at a time, but owing to my schedule, I frequently had to stay longer than I had hoped. The sorrow of being apart from my family was intense, as was a searing ache in my jaw. This soreness has been coming and going for a while, but it got worse while I was in LA. I found a beautiful dentist who was unable to determine what was wrong but advised me to return if the condition persisted. I flew back to London and had a wisdom teeth out on the advise of my dentist, as we both thought it was too close to the next tooth and that food was getting lodged between them, causing the difficulty. (I apologize for the terrible image in any book, much less a culinary memoir.) However, the pain worsened after the removal. Back in Los Angeles, I visited my old dentist, who examined me and suggested that I had oral cancer. I was really surprised and passed out. Kate died after a harrowing four-year fight with cancer, and the notion of returning to her surroundings horrified me. My dentist urged me to get a scan right away. I was going that evening and decided to have it done in the United Kingdom.

I postponed the appointment due to trepidation and a truly haughty denial that I might ever develop cancer. The pain lasted for some time and increased. This caused me to start taking Ibuprofen on a regular basis.

As the pain worsened and my ibuprofen dosage increased, I continued to work, but it got increasingly difficult. I returned to London with greater agony than before after working in Toronto around Christmas 2017. Felicity insisted that I consult a doctor in London who specialised in salivary gland cancer. "You have a huge tumour at the base of your tongue," he said within ten seconds of forcing my lips wide with a gloved hand and staring down my throat. This is what you will do because it is almost certainly cancerous. You will receive a scan. This scan will most likely show whether you have cancer and whether it has spread. Then, if possible, surgery will be used to remove it. Then you'll get radiation and chemotherapy, and you may have to eat through a feeding tube in your stomach for a period." To say the least, he lacked bedside manners. I nearly passed out again.

We had traveled around the world in search of a cure for Kate, and we had met a number of doctors and scientists, some traditional, some alternative, who had dedicated their lives to finding a cure for what Siddhartha Mukherjee refers to as the emperor of all maladies, so I had learned about cancer from a variety of perspectives, and that knowledge had made me both hopeful and terrified. Because Kate's experience with standard of care (chemotherapy, radiation, etc.) had been so horrific and ultimately ineffective, I was determined not to go through it myself.

The problem was that because the tumor was so massive, surgery would have required removing a large section of my tongue, assuring that I would never be able to eat or talk normally again. As a result, the only viable option was 35 days of high-dose targeted radiation, followed by seven sessions of low-dose chemotherapy. Fortunately, because the disease had miraculously not spread, it had been established that using this treatment resulted in a cure rate of about 90% with an extremely low recurrence rate. These were challenging figures to disagree with. So, ultimately, I did it because I had no choice. Of course, I was scared, and despite being such a proactive and positive force, I knew Felicity was, too. And deservedly so. She was pregnant, we were preparing to move into a new home, and we had a two-year-old and three high school-aged kids. Nonetheless, her intrinsic tenacity, determination, and intelligence in determining the best course of action and locating the most experienced, cutting-edge team of professionals whose therapies would ensure a successful outcome surpassed whatever concerns she may have had. Her support, kindness, and patience were and continue to be pillars of strength for me in all aspects of medicine and life. Unfortunately, she doesn't feel the same way about me.

Dr. Eric Genden, the department chairman at Mount Sinai Hospital in New York City, devised the original treatment plan, and Dr. Richard Bakst took over my care from there. When I met him, it was evident that Dr. Bakst had received an extra dose of bedside manner after graduating from medical school. Regardless matter how polite and supportive he and his colleagues were, my main concern was that one of the most important and critical areas of my life would or could be seriously injured, potentially forever. That essential component is the ability to taste, eat, and appreciate food.

How could they expect me to purposely lose my sense of smell and taste, as well as endure the humiliation of being fed through a tube in my stomach, both of which I was anxious to avoid? They listened attentively as I communicated my concern through a series of questions, to which they always responded that, yes, it would be difficult, and I would lose my sense of taste and smell, as well as most of my saliva, but that I would most likely recover completely in time. They didn't convince me. But I did it. Except for the occasions when I didn't.

THE TREATMENT

To receive targeted radiation to the neck or head, the patient's head must be completely immobile. A custom-made webbed mask would be placed over my face, neck, and upper part of my shoulders five days a week for seven weeks, then strapped to a board to completely immobilize my head during the sessions. To keep my mouth and tongue as still as possible, a "bite block" was inserted through a hole in the mask and held between my teeth. I was beginning to realize that, for better or worse, the majority of critical influences in my life entered through this orifice. After three treatments, I developed labyrinthitis, which I had previously had on occasion. It is a severe form of vertigo that produces nausea and prevents you from doing anything but lying down until it passes. Unfortunately, it also caused me to lose my appetite, precisely as the radiation began to affect my taste buds, salivary glands, and the flora and soft tissue in my mouth. After a week of treatments, anything I could put in my mouth tasted like old, damp cardboard. After a few days, everything tasted like wet cardboard splattered with someone's garbage. Ulcers erupted in my mouth, as did thick, foul-tasting saliva. Everything above deteriorated steadily from that point on. The fragrance of any food revolted me since it did not smell like what it was supposed to smell like. If I tried to put anything in my mouth at this point, all I could smell or taste was the worst culinary ingredients. My inability to consume anything save beef or chicken broth remained. I attempted to find something to eat in the fridge, but when I opened the door, I was met by foul odors. Because, as previously indicated, I could only smell the most unpleasant aspects of any given object, every carrot, carton of milk, orange, and leftover roasted chicken sitting innocently in the fridge combined into a foul wall of odor. I tried a few more times before giving up on the fridge and, finally, the entire kitchen. If Felicity, who was very pregnant but as strong as ever at this point, entered the bedroom where I lay in a profound state of nausea, unable to even read, and if she had just eaten or cooked something, the odours that clung to her were so powerfully repellent to me that I would ask her to stand at a distance for fear of vomiting all over herself. I was given protein drinks, which I couldn't even finish. The morphine I was given to help me sleep and mask the pain created such severe constipation that I believed it could only be treated with a small pipe bomb. The irony was that I was watching cooking shows while undergoing chemo treatments once a week or IV fluids to keep me hydrated in the hospital. "WTF?!" they exclaim or tweet. This was pure masochism on my part, as the idea of food repulsed me. In retrospect, I suppose it was a way for me to hang on to what I loved or remember what I had once had because I was desperate to have it back. I was determined to heal faster than any patient before me. Whatever the doctors or statistics said, I would regain my sense of taste and saliva sooner rather than later by watching MasterChef, Giada De Laurentiis, Iron Chef, Diners, Drive-Ins, and Dives, and that disgusting, unnecessary show with the guy who eats as much of something as possible for no apparent reason and yet somehow still lives, because they were the fuel that would get me there.

Felicity gave birth to Emilia on April 19, while still undergoing chemotherapy. She was delivered by caesarean section, which, as we all know, is best for the baby but not so great for the mother for quite some time afterward, but vaginal birth is also not a spectacular experience. (Let's be honest, if men had to give birth, the world would probably only have 47 people instead of billions, and abortion clinics would be just another department at Walmart alongside auto parts, golf equipment, and weapons.) Fortunately, I was well enough to attend the birth and see Felicity and our beloved issue thereafter, but I soon had to return to my bed. I kept hoping to regain enough strength to hold Emilia and help Felicity, but by the fifth week, I was so unwell, queasy, and underweight that I practically begged to have a feeding tube installed into my stomach. That tube was meant to be in my body for around six months. By the end of my therapy, I had lost thirty pounds (about two stone), lost all of my facial and neck hair, and could hardly walk up a flight of stairs. When we returned to London, I had to stay in bed all day and feed myself through a tube, either with protein smoothies or, eventually, my own meals. I'd missed cooking so much that I'd fight the smell of the ingredients just to be able to stand at the stove and prepare something I knew I could eat. It didn't matter what it tasted like because it was going straight into my stomach via the tube, but it was critical to me that if someone else ate it by mouth, they would find it appealing. I'd purée beans and chicken stock with spaghetti or egg fried rice, but I'd need to thin it up with water or more stock to keep the tube from clogging. I also used the tube to stay hydrated because drinking water via my mouth hurt like battery acid. When I told my oldest children, Nicolo, Isabel, and Camilla, about my declining health, they were upbeat and encouraging. However, I realized how terrible it was for them to see me in such poor health when their mother had suffered similarly not even a decade before. It was evident that my cancer diagnosis worried them, but Felicity and I persuaded them that my prognosis was much different from Kate's. However, the trauma of losing a parent never fully resolves. This is something only the parent can accomplish. I realized that no matter how much reassurance we gave them, some of them feared having to go through that catastrophe again.

Week after week, month after month, as Matteo's height and vocabulary grew, Emilia began to sleep through the night and crawl, Nico and Isabel applied to universities and graduated high school, Camilla approached her junior year, we moved into our new home, Felicity recovered from surgery, and I gradually improved.

However, I must say that the recuperation was more longer and more difficult than I had anticipated. I had been depressed during treatment and for several months afterward. Many days, I felt like a ghost in my own home, confined to my bed, listening to my family go about their lives downstairs while I was unable to contribute in any way. There were times when I feared I'd never be able to cook or share a meal with those I care about again. I flew to New York City for a scan six months after my previous treatment and stayed with our friends Ryan Reynolds and Blake Lively. (I apologize for smashing your rice bowl if you thought the name-dropping had stopped.) I wanted to go to the scan alone, but Ryan insisted on accompanying me. (He is the only obnoxious Canadian I know.) The doctors gathered to discuss the morning's scan results, which revealed "no evidence of disease" (my new fave four words in any language). Needless to say, I was thrilled. Ryan and the female doctors were both in tears, but I knew it was because they were so close to him. I was pleased when the doctors unanimously decided that I could finally take the feeding tube out of my torso. A water-filled balloon prevents the tube from dropping out of you and onto the floor; to remove it, simply empty the balloon, hold the tube, and yank, which I was told felt like a punch in the gut. I inquired whether we might do it straight away rather than waiting for the doctor who had inserted it. Dr. Bakst approved the removal of the indecorous appendage since the mood was positive as a result of the good news and Mr. Reynolds' presence in the room. One of the female doctors, who, like the rest of the staff, even the men, had been flushed since Deadpool's arrival, consented to perform the task. She had seized the tube and was about to tear it from my fragile torso when I cried, "Wait!"

"What?!" she said, slightly annoyed that I had spoilt her big moment in front of you-know-who.

"Don't you want to deflate the balloon first?"

"The…?"

"It's the balloon." I said to myself. You must… or it will not fit through the—"

"Oh, yeah, yeah." Yes. Without a question. Sorry. "I just…" "I have not done it in a long time."

She completed the procedure correctly, amidst much laughter, and I was finally free of what had been my second mouth for far too long. I felt a fantastic sense of liberty after the tube was removed. Now I had no alternative but to eat via the orifice designed particularly for that purpose. Although I had begun eating by mouth, my diet was restricted to soft, moderate foods. This was disappointing, but I knew I'd been extraordinarily fortunate not to have lost my ability to swallow properly or move my tongue normally, both of which are typical side effects even without surgery because radiation may cause severe damage to the muscles required for both acts. In post-treatment programs, speech therapists provide specialized exercises to recuperating patients to help them regain tongue and jaw movement. Fortunately, four years of speech and vocal training had made me acutely aware of what was going on, and I was able to perform the necessary actions to maintain normal movement along the way.

My mouth had been exceedingly sensitive for almost two years. I couldn't drink fizzy drinks or eat hot foods. I could drink and taste alcohol, although I usually drank white wine with plenty of ice. The tannins in red wine made my mouth feel like someone had dragged a cloth covered in dust and pepper across it, so it needed to be chilled. Martinis were a horrible fight for me. Steak was impossible because a lack of saliva prevents the meat from being broken down enough to swallow, resulting in a bolus that is easily choked on. (I had a few near-misses while trying to eat something as simple as a chicken breast.) The same could be said for most meats and large slices of bread. Whatever I ate had to have moisture in it or around it, or else it took a long time to pass through my throat or I couldn't consume it at all.

The human body is amazingly well-balanced. With a little less saliva, the amount of food that can be swallowed decreases significantly. I was envious of my family members' ability to grab a piece of bread or cracker, a bit of smoked salmon, or a couple slices of salami to place on a baguette and gulp it down without thinking. I'd have to figure out how much to add to everything I put in my mouth to avoid choking. I used to eat way too quickly, exactly like my father. As a child, I would eat my second dish of pasta before my sisters finished their first. This heinous habit vanished due to necessity. I couldn't even speak to someone across the table while eating. For the most part, I had to do the task at hand before participating in the discussion.

Even when I was able to eat out, have people over for dinner, or go to someone else's house for supper, I was nervous because I didn't know what I'd be able to eat. I was scared that I'd choke on something or eat something spicy by accident, leaving me unable to eat for the rest of the night owing to the agony in my mouth. If someone asked me to try something, whether it was a friend, a restaurant owner, or a chef, I would take a bite only to be polite and pretend that I could taste, swallow, or wasn't in agony. They couldn't understand or envision how something so tasty could taste like garbage to me, or how even mild spices could irritate my tongue for the following 24 hours, or how it felt to consume anything with nearly no saliva. Even at home, I found myself eating separately from my family because I was embarrassed by how difficult it was for me to finish a simple bowl of pasta. All of this was frustrating and opposed to how I had lived my life since birth.

I usually socialised by eating and drinking. Although there was some progress each week, I couldn't help but believe that things would never return to the way they were when life was edible.

As previously said, I ate mostly vegetarian for almost two years, with the exception of stocks and broths. The following dish was a staple because it was quick to prepare and contained all of the nutrients I needed to keep healthy. I can honestly say that even after all this time, I'm still not tired of it since it's so delicious. This recipe, along with scrambled eggs, oatmeal, and various soups, effectively sustained me and helped me restore my strength.

Chapter 12.

THE END

THANK YOU.

As I write this, I am almost completely cured. (I ate venison the other night, albeit at a slower pace than normal, but I ate it and enjoyed it.) Thank you to Dr. Bakst and his staff, particularly Bethann Scarborough, Mount Sinai's chief of palliative care; my friends and family; and, most significantly, my wife, Felicity Blunt. After two and a half years of scans, workouts, and tons of beans, I now have a clean bill of health. Fortunately, after three years, the chances of this type of cancer returning are extremely low, and the chances of it ever reappearing decrease substantially with each passing year. I'd also like to thank Dr. Niven Narain from BERG for his help getting me through it all.

Throughout my rehabilitation, I was extremely lucky to have our nanny, Martina Domanicka, and my assistant, Lottie Birmingham, in New York with me, Felicity, and Matteo, and Andrea Galik in London with Nicolo, Isabel, and Camilla. All three of those women went above and beyond to assist us get through what I hope will be our most difficult time. Felicity would not have been able to care for a newborn and a bedridden husband while mending without the help of my dear in-laws Joanna, Oliver, Susie, and Sebastian. Despite the fact that

Felicity was supposed to be on maternity leave, she continued to work from home, believing she was abdicating her responsibilities to her clients. She was, and still is, unstoppable. I hope that my "showbiz" agents and management are reading and taking notes. But I am joking. I'd also like to thank the agents and Tony, my manager, for their patience and encouragement.

How can I compensate my parents for their unfailing support and visits after Emilia's birth? I'm sure seeing me so frail was distressing for them. Thank you also to my sister Gina, who came to see me during treatment to cheer me up, and to my sister Christine, who was always positive and supportive from her home in Los Angeles.

Thank you also to my lovely friend Alison Benson, who hosted me when I first arrived in New York for my initial testing, as well as my cousin Joe and his wife Robin. Emily and John, my sister-in-law and brother-in-law, graciously allowed us to stay in their lovely Westchester home throughout my treatment, ironically close to where I was raised and from where we had only moved four years prior. This was a selfless act worthy of sainthood. (Because I've been told I can't directly beatify someone, I've made a few international calls. Brexit appears to have made things more difficult, but I'm working on it.

Ryan Reynolds and Blake Lively, who offered us their outrageously elegant New York apartment for two weeks when Felicity was in labor so we could be closer to the hospital. And I'm not sure how to thank Ryan for accompanying me on the day of my first scan. I was, and still am, pleased that he was present. During the same two weeks, Martina and Lottie were fostered by our dear friends Oliver Platt and Camilla. I am not sure what we would have done without their generosity.

Many friends visited me in the hospital or on weekends to lift my spirits, which was no easy task, but I'm sure it made the doctors and nurses very glad to see a parade of well-known beloved actors wandering up and down the ward on occasion.

When I returned to London, a man like Colin Firth would almost everyday check in on me, drive me to the hospital for checkups, and sit with me for hydration. His support proved crucial.

When I was allowed to resume exercising, our friend and Pilates instructor Monique Eastwood, as well as our trainer Daryll Martin, gently helped me rebuild muscle and return to the level of fitness I had previously achieved, and then some!

How can such goodness be repaid?

I suppose I will find out.

Surprisingly, some of them have been stopping over around dinnertime lately.

For them, everything revolves around eating.

Gluttons.

Chapter 13.

COOKING RECIPES

— A NEGRONI UP —

50 millilitres gin

25 millimetres Campari

25 millimetres good sweet vermouth

Ice

1 orange slice

- Pour all the booze into a cocktail shaker filled with ice.
- Shake it well.
- Strain it into a coupe.
- Garnish with a slice of orange.
- Sit down.
- Drink it.
- The sun is now in your stomach.

— PASTA CON AGLIO E OLIO —

3 garlic cloves, quartered

14 cup extra virgin olive oil

1 lb. spaghetti

freshly ground black pepper and kosher salt

Paprika

- Cook the garlic in olive oil until it is gently browned.
- Cook the spaghetti till al dente.
- Toss the spaghetti with the oil and garlic mixture.
- Season with salt, pepper, and paprika to taste.
- Cheese is not allowed.

— TROPIANO BOTTLED TOMATO SAUCE —

Bushels of tomatoes (you decide how many)
Salt
Fresh basil
One outdoor open fireplace or fire pit, with heavy metal grates
Fire
Two large galvanised aluminium tubs
One white pillowcase
Lots of old long-necked glass soda bottles
One ladle
One funnel
Lots of new soda bottle caps
One bottle-capping device
One thick piece of oilcloth big enough to cover one of the tubs
Enough water to fill one of the tubs

- Start the fire.
- Fill one tub with water and place it on the fire grate.
- Take a bunch of tomatoes, stuff them into the pillowcase, and squeeze the s#*! out of them over the other tub, allowing the tomato juice to flow through the weave of the pillowcase, making it look like a remnant of the Saint Valentine's Day

Massacre. Continue until all of the tomatoes have been consumed, or until you feel like Macbeth at the conclusion of his play.
- Fill the bottles (by funnel) with tomato juice one at a time, finishing with a sprinkling of salt and a basil leaf.
- Close the bottles.
- Place the bottles in the water in the other tub.
- Wrap them with the oilcloth.
- Boil them for a few minutes. (I'm not sure what the health ruling is on this, so/and/but I accept no responsibility for any foodborne infections).
- Take the bottles out.
- Allow them to cool.
- Put them in my grandfather's wine cellar, or store them somewhere cool and dry that is more convenient for you.

Throughout the year, this sauce was utilized. It was light and sweet, and it could be made with olive oil, sautéed garlic and onions, or as preferred. For months of red gold, one or two long days of work are required. The bottles would be stored on wooden shelves in the wine cellar, beside mason jars of pickled green tomatoes or roasted peppers marinated in olive oil and seasoned with salt and a single clove of garlic. Small homemade salami and waxy, pear-shaped provolone cheese bulbs hung from the wooden rafters above the vacuum-sealed treasures.

So we must return to the wine cellar. Yes, we must return to the must. When one entered the wine cellar, the must was overwhelming. Must and mildew, dark and thick, covered everything, including the antique wine press in the corner. Following the first breath, it was clear that new life forms were emerging from the spores that danced on every surface, including one's nostrils and lungs. However, the joy my grandfather had in drawing his vinified love from the foetid oak barrel into the abraded decanter and delivering it to my father or uncles (and subsequently, myself and my cousins) more than compensated for any respiratory diseases we were sure to catch. It was an honour to be invited to participate in, or simply observe, the wine cellar ceremony. In fact, I was outraged when my sisters begged to accompany me since I saw this as a distinctly male rite of passage. Those of us present were filled with pride as the hazy purple wine was carried upstairs to the table in its decanter, poured into juice glasses, toasted, and sipped heartily.

— TOMATO SALAD —

8 small ripe tomatoes (quartered or halved, depending upon their size)

1 garlic clove, halved

A glug of EVOO

A small handful of basil leaves, torn

A splash of red wine vinegar (optional)

Coarse salt

- Combine the tomatoes, garlic, olive oil, basil, and vinegar, if using, in a mixing bowl. Toss.
- A few minutes before serving, season with salt. (If you add it too soon, the water in the tomatoes may evaporate, diluting the dish.)
- The corn on the cob was boiled for about six minutes before being placed on a huge dish and served to the table steaming hot. Greedy hands then took hold of heated ears. But buttering the corn wasn't as simple as "put knife into butter, put butter on corn with knife."
- No. No.
- Thank you, God.

- No.
- In true Italian fashion, a piece of homemade bread was buttered and then used to slather the salted ear of corn, resulting in two dishes from one, the ear of corn being the first and the homemade bread (now saturated with the melted butter, salt, and sweetness from the buttered kernels) being the second. This was possibly the most wonderful element of an already delicious meal. An almost stupidly basic act. Except for my family, no one I know does it. And, as far as I am aware, they are neither simple nor foolish. (Perhaps one or two.) I can only recommend that the next time you eat corn on the cob, try the above, and you'll see what I mean.

— RAGÙ TUCCI —

This is the traditional way the Tuccis make ragù. My maternal grandmother made a lighter version of this same sauce. It calls for spareribs and stewing beef in this recipe, but different cuts of meat may be added depending on what is on hand—pork chops, sausage, pig's feet. It is delicious with polpette (meatballs), which may be added to the sauce during the last half hour of cooking. The sauce may be prepared two days ahead of serving. Refrigerate it overnight and reheat before tossing with the pasta. It may also be frozen with the meat and meatballs.

¼ cup olive oil

1 pound stewing beef, trimmed of fat, rinsed, patted dry, and cut into medium-size pieces

1 pound country-style spareribs, trimmed of fat, cut in half, rinsed, and patted dry

1 cup roughly chopped onions

3 garlic cloves, roughly chopped

½ cup dry red wine

One 6-ounce can tomato paste

1 ½ cups warm water, plus more as needed

8 cups canned whole plum tomatoes (about two 35-ounce cans), passed through a food mill or pureed in the blender

3 fresh basil leaves

1 tablespoon fresh oregano leaves, chopped, or 1 teaspoon dried

- Warm the olive oil in a stew pot set over medium-high heat. Sear the stewing beef until brown on all sides, about 10 minutes. Remove from the pot and set aside in a bowl. Add the spare ribs to the pot and sear until they are brown on all sides, about 10 minutes. Remove the ribs and set aside in the bowl with the stewing beef. (If your pot is big enough to hold all the meat in a single layer, it may be cooked at the same time.)
- Stir the onions and garlic into the pot. Reduce the heat to low and cook until the onions begin to soften and lose their shape, about 5 minutes. Stir in the wine, scraping the bottom of the pot clean. Add the tomato paste. Pour ½ cup of the warm water into the can to loosen any residual paste and then pour the water into the pot. Cook to warm the paste through, about 2 minutes. Add the tomatoes along with the remaining 1 cup warm water. Stir in the basil and oregano. Cover with the lid slightly askew and simmer to sweeten the tomatoes, about 30 minutes.
- Return the meat to the pot along with any juices that have accumulated in the bowl. Cover with the lid slightly askew and simmer, stirring frequently, until the meat is very tender and the tomatoes are cooked, about 2 hours. Warm water may be added to the sauce, in ½-cup portions, if the sauce becomes too

thick. (If you have made meatballs, they may be added during the last half hour of cooking. The meatballs will soften and absorb some of the sauce.)

— SPAGHETTI WITH LENTILS —

½ carrot, finely chopped

½ onion, finely chopped

½ stalk celery, finely chopped

½ garlic clove, sliced

3 tablespoons extra-virgin olive oil, plus more for drizzling

1 cup dried brown lentils, rinsed and picked over

½ pound spaghetti

1 ½ cups salsa marinara

Salt

Freshly ground black pepper

- In a medium or large saucepan (big enough to hold all of the ingredients, including the pasta), sauté the carrot, onion, celery, and garlic in the olive oil over medium-low heat until tender, about 7 minutes.
- In a separate medium saucepan, place the lentils. Fill the pan 1 inch over the lentils with cold water. Bring to a simmer and boil for 20 minutes, or until the lentils are barely soft. Set aside after removing from the heat.
- To break the spaghetti, spread out a clean dish towel, wrap it around the spaghetti, and fold the ends over. Roll, squeeze,

and/or bend this bundle until the spaghetti has broken down into 1- to 1-and-a-half-inch pieces. Place the bundle over a wide basin and unroll it to empty it of all the spaghetti crumbs.
- A big saucepan of salted water should be brought to a boil. Cook until the spaghetti is al dente.
- Before draining the pasta, save 12 cups of the cooking water.
- Meanwhile, rinse the lentils and add them to the sautéed vegetables in the pot. Mix in the marinara salsa. Bring to a simmer, cover, and cook for 10 minutes, or until the lentils have merged with the sauce. To make a liquid consistency, add the drained pasta and the leftover pasta water. Season to taste with salt and pepper. Simmer the noodles and sauce together for 3 minutes to allow the flavours to blend. Serve right away.
- In terms of meatballs, I believe that good ground beef with a fair bit of fat, combined with an almost one-to-one meat/bread ratio, is the secret to a fantastic one. Stale Italian or French white bread, crusts removed, should be soaked in water and filtered. According to this palate, meatballs should be renamed "meat-bread balls" or "breatballs"—or something similar but not as stupid—because the proper ratio of both ingredients is the secret to their success.

— TIMPANO —

The timpano dough is flattened out into a thin round, the diameter of which is dictated by the baking pan. Add the bottom of the pan's diameter, the top of the pan's diameter, and twice the height of the pan. The sum will be the approximate diameter required. The dough can be kneaded ahead of time and left aside while the pan is prepared, or it can be chilled overnight. Allow it to come back to room temperature before rolling it out. Before you line the pan with the dough, generously lubricate it with butter and olive oil. While the pasta is cooking, grease and line the pan with the dough.

Because no one has room for anything other than salad after eating timpano, the meat used in the ragù is usually served for supper the night before the timpano is cooked.

FOR THE DOUGH

4 cups all-purpose flour, plus more for dusting

4 large eggs

1 teaspoon kosher salt

3 tablespoons olive oil

½ cup water

TO PREPARE THE PAN

Butter

Olive oil

3 pounds ziti, cooked very al dente (about half the time recommended on the package) and drained (18 cups cooked)

2 tablespoons olive oil

8 cups Ragù Tucci (double the recipe on page 71), at room temperature

4 cups (¼ x ½-inch pieces) Genoa salami, at room temperature

4 cups (¼ x ½-inch cubes) sharp provolone cheese, at room temperature

12 hard-boiled large eggs, shelled, quartered lengthwise, and each quarter cut in half to create chunks, at room temperature

4 cups little meatballs, at room temperature

1 cup finely grated Pecorino Romano

6 large eggs, beaten

To prepare the dough, follow these steps: In a stand mixer with a dough hook attachment, combine the flour, eggs, salt, and olive oil. (A larger food processor can also be used.) Mix in 3 tablespoons of water. Add more water, 1 tablespoon at a time, until the dough forms a ball. Turn the dough out onto a lightly floured surface and knead for 10 minutes to ensure it is thoroughly mixed. Set aside 5 minutes to rest.

(To create the dough by hand, first mix together the flour and salt on a clean, dry work surface or pastry board. Create a pile of dry ingredients and a well in the center. Break the eggs into the center of the well and beat lightly with a fork. Add 3 tablespoons of water at this point. Using a fork, gradually stir some of the dry ingredients into the egg mixture. Continue to combine the dry ingredients with the eggs, adding 1 tablespoon of the remaining water at a time. Knead the dough with your hands until it is thoroughly combined, smooth, and dry. If the dough becomes too sticky, add extra flour. Set aside 5 minutes to rest.

Flatten out the dough on a lightly floured surface. Dust the top of the dough with flour and roll it out until it is about 116 inches thick and the desired diameter, sprinkling flour and flipping the dough over occasionally to keep it from sticking to the work surface.

To prepare the pan, follow these steps: Make sure the timpano baking pan (a round enamel basin or casserole dish) is thoroughly oiled with butter and olive oil. Fold the dough in half again to make a triangle, and place it in the pan. Unfold the dough and place it in the pan, gently pressing it against the bottom and edges and draping any excess dough over the edge. Set aside.

Preheat the oven to 350 °F.

Prepare the filling. Toss the drained pasta with olive oil and let aside for a few minutes before mixing in 2 cups of the ragù. Four heaping cups of spaghetti should be spread over the dough at the bottom of the timpano. Add 1 cup salami, 1 cup provolone, 3 hard-boiled eggs, 1 cup meatballs, and 13 cups Romano cheese. Two cups of ragù should be poured over these ingredients. Repeat this procedure to create further layers, using an equal amount of each ingredient until they reach 1 inch from the pan's lip, and top with 2 cups of ragù.

Over the filling, pour the beaten eggs. Fold the dough over the filling to create a perfect seal. Any overlapping dough should be cut and thrown. Make sure the timpano is properly closed. If you find any minor gaps, cut a piece of trimmed dough to fit over the opening, moistening the scraps with a little water to ensure a tight seal.

Bake for an hour or until lightly browned. Cover with aluminum foil and bake for 30 minutes, or until the dough is golden brown and the timpano is thoroughly cooked. Remove from the oven and let cool and contract for 30 minutes before removing from the pan. (The baked timpano should not adhere to the pan. To test, gently shake the pan from left to right. The pan should spin slightly. If any components are still connected, carefully remove them using a knife.

To remove the timpano from the pan, place it on top of a baking sheet or thin cutting board large enough to span the whole circumference of the pan. Invert the timpano by firmly gripping the baking sheet or cutting board and the pan's rim. Remove the pan and let the timpano cool for an additional 30 minutes.

Cut a 3 inch circle in the center of the timpano with a long, sharp knife, making sure to get all the way to the bottom. Then, like a pie, cut the timpano into individual bits, leaving the middle circle as a base for the rest pieces. The sliced pieces should remain intact, exhibiting the wonderful material that has been accumulated over time.

— A CHRISTMAS COCKTAIL —

1 tablespoon pomegranate seeds

50 millilitres Ketel One vodka

25 millimetres Cointreau

25 millimetres cranberry juice (either unsweetened or cranberry juice cocktail; your preference)

25 millimetres pomegranate juice

Ice

1 raspberry, mint leaf, and fresh rosemary sprig, to garnish

- Muddle the pomegranate seeds in a shaker until they are mixed.

- Pour in the alcohol.
- Pour in the juices.
- Pour in the ice.
- Shake things up.
- Pour into a coupe or Martini glass.
- Garnish with a raspberry wrapped in a mint leaf and impaled on a rosemary stalk. Drink it to make your holiday happier.

— PIZZOCCHERI —

1 medium Savoy cabbage

A big, sexy slab of Valtellina cheese, or something similar, like fontina

3 large yellow potatoes

A fuck of a lot of butter

4 large garlic cloves

1 pound pizzoccheri

Extra-virgin olive oil

2 handfuls grated Parmigiano-Reggiano, or Bitto (if available and you can afford it)

Salt

- Remove and remove any tough outer leaves from the cabbage, then coarsely slice it into long pieces. Cut around 15 slices of Valtellina cheese thinly and grate about 3 cups. Set aside.
- Preheat the oven to 325°F.
- Peel and dice the potatoes and boil until tender but still firm, about 15 minutes. Add the cabbage to the potatoes halfway

through cooking. When the potatoes and cabbage are done, rinse them and set them aside.
- Melt the butter in a big, deep frying pan over low heat. Gently crush (if possible) the garlic cloves, set them in the pan, and cook until softened and the butter has melted but not gone brown.
- Boil the pizzoccheri until al dente, then drain, reserving about 2 cups of the water. Return the pizzoccheri to the pot and sprinkle with olive oil or butter to keep them from sticking together. Pour a little of the garlic butter into a baking dish and begin layering the ingredients, beginning with the pizzoccheri, then the cabbage, then the potatoes, then both cheeses, drizzling more garlic butter over the whole mixture after each layer, adding a bit of the reserved pasta water to ensure it doesn't get too thick but not too watery. You may only require a cup. Finish with a sprinkle of olive oil and additional grated cheese.
- Cover with foil and bake for about 15 minutes. Remove the foil and return to the oven until the top is slightly crisp. Season to taste.
- Serve it, eat it, and drink a lot of wine with it, thinking about how much you deserve it since you burned off so many calories being so active in the chilly outdoors.

— FRITTATA —

5 or 6 large eggs

3 to 4 tablespoons olive oil

Kosher salt

A good pinch of chopped fresh flat-leaf parsley (optional)

A good pinch of freshly grated Parmigiano-Reggiano

Freshly ground black pepper

- Crack the eggs into a bowl and beat them gently with a fork for a minute or so, making sure you angle the bowl so that you really blend them well. You could use a whisk instead of a fork, if you prefer, but you will end up with a puffier-textured frittata.
- In a 10-inch sauté pan with sloping sides, heat the olive oil over medium-high heat. You want to get it pretty hot and tilt the pan to make sure the sides are well coated. When the oil is hot, season the eggs with salt and add the parsley, if using, then pour the mixture into the pan. Scramble the eggs vigorously with a silicone spatula, tipping and moving the pan continuously and drawing the eggs from the sides into the middle. Keep the pan moving to make sure the eggs don't stick. Add the Parmigiano and a good grinding of pepper. Then flip or turn the frittata and cook for a minute or so more, until golden and cooked through. Serve immediately.

A PAUSE FOR A LIBATION: THE OLD-FASHIONED

This mythical libation, purportedly created in 1806 in upstate New York, was the first drink to be referred to as a "cocktail." Water, Whisky, Bitters, and Sugar. That was pretty much it. By the middle of the century, the cocktail had gotten more sophisticated, with the addition of diverse liquors like orange curaçao, absinthe, and who knows what else. Drinkers seeking a simpler version would request that it be prepared "the old-fashioned way," giving origin to the drink's now-famous name. I'm not a big lover of bourbon, but this cocktail is irresistible.

- 1 teaspoon simple syrup
- A few dashes Angostura bitters
- 2 shots rye or bourbon
- Ice
- Orange slice and cherry, to garnish
- Pour the simple syrup into an "old-fashioned glass," meaning a rocks glass.
- Add the Angostura bitters.
- Add the booze.
- Add the ice.
- Stir.
- Add the garnish.
- You could also make this with scotch, or Irish whiskey if you prefer.

— PINO POSTERARO'S PARMIGIANO STOCK —

Pino Posteraro's Parmigiano Stock

1 quart water

1 large Parmigiano rind (about 1 ½ pounds)

7 ounces coarse sea salt

3 small bay leaves

- Fill a large pot with the water. Wrap the rind in cheesecloth, tie tightly with string, and secure to the side of the pot (this helps avoid the Parmigiano's sinking to the bottom of the pot and burning). Submerge the wrapped rind.
- Add the salt and bay leaves.
- Gently boil for 2 hours, strain, and use for Bolognese.

— PINO POSTERARO FETTUCCINE WITH RAGU ALLA BOLOGNESE —

1 tablespoon onions, chopped

1 tablespoon carrots, chopped

1 tablespoon celery, chopped

2 tablespoons extra-virgin olive oil

1 ounce mixed fresh herbs (such as rosemary, sage, and/or thyme), chopped

2 bay leaves

2 ounces dried porcini mushrooms, reconstituted

½ pound lean ground beef or veal

1 ounce tomato paste

3 ½ tablespoons dry white wine

3 ½ tablespoons freshly squeezed orange juice

1 tablespoon salt

A pinch of black pepper

1 ¼ pints chicken stock (or Parmigiano stock, opposite)

1 pint beef jus (or Parmigiano stock)

10 ounces egg fettuccine

1 ounce butter

1 ounce 36% fat whipping cream (optional)

1 ¼ ounces Grana Padano, grated

- In a large saucepan over medium heat, sweat the vegetables in the olive oil with the herbs and porcini. Add the meat and cook until brown, perhaps utilising a lid to achieve a better and faster result. Add the tomato paste, wine, and orange juice and let the liquids evaporate. Add the salt, pepper, and stocks and let simmer for about 1 ½ hours.
- When the ragout is cooked, boil the fettuccine in salted water until al dente. Add the butter and the cream, if using, to the ragu alla Bolognese, toss the pasta with the sauce, and sprinkle with the grated Grana Padano.

— THE MARTINI —

Ice

Dry vermouth

Gin or vodka

Olives or a lemon twist, to garnish

- Take a glass beaker and fill it with ice.
- Pour in a half shot of good dry vermouth.
- Stir it well for about 15 seconds.
- Let it sit for about 30 seconds.
- Stir it again.
- Strain out the vermouth.
- Pour in 3 to 4 shots of good gin or good vodka.
- Stir it well for about 30 seconds.
- Let it sit for about 30 seconds.
- Stir it again for another 30 seconds.
- Let it sit for another 30 seconds.
- Stir it quickly.
- Strain it into a chilled glass.
- Garnish with either 1 or 3 olives (never 2) or a lemon twist.
- Drink it.
- Become a new person.

— FELICITY'S "RULE, BRITANNIA!" ROAST POTATOES —

2 pounds russet potatoes, peeled and cut into 2-inch pieces

Kosher salt

2 to 3 tablespoons vegetable oil or goose fat

- Preheat the oven to 400°F.
- Place the potatoes in a large saucepan with a pinch of salt and add enough water to cover. Bring the water to a boil and parboil the potatoes for about 10 minutes. (Do not overcook them—otherwise you will end up with mush at the next step. The outside needs to be just soft enough to be scored with a fork.) Drain the potatoes and return them to the pan. Put a lid on the pan and shake the hell out of it, breaking up and fluffing the outside of the potato pieces. Set aside.
- Pour the oil or fat into a metal or enamel roasting pan and place it in the oven until it's really hot. Remove the pan from the oven and place it on the stovetop over low heat. Put the potatoes in the oil and turn them in it several times to coat. Then roast them in the oven for a good hour, turning them twice during the cooking time.

— FISH STEW —

2 pounds fresh mussels (the smaller the better)

2 pounds fresh vongole (small clams)

¼ cup sea salt or cornmeal

1 teaspoon saffron threads (optional)

2 cups warm or room-temperature shrimp stock (optional, but it gives a richer flavour)

2 cups warm or room-temperature fish stock (if using shrimp stock; if not using shrimp stock as well, have 4 cups ready)

Extra-virgin olive oil

4 garlic cloves, halved

1 medium onion, diced

4 cups chopped fresh tomatoes

3 basil leaves, torn in half

Sea salt

2 whole pepperoncini (optional)

2 cups white wine

Freshly ground black pepper

12 medium shrimp, shells on

1 pound fresh cod (or similar fish), cut into small chunks

1 pound fresh monkfish (or similar fish), cut into small chunks

A handful of fresh parsley, chopped

Good toasted bread, for serving

- Wash and pull the "beards" off the mussels.
- Place the vongole and mussels into separate bowls of cold water, add the salt or cornmeal, and leave to purge for about an hour.
- After the mussels and vongole have purged, place half of each into a large frying pan of boiling salted water and cover for a few minutes until they have opened. Then remove the meat

from the shells, place it into a bowl, and set aside. Discard the shells.
- Sprinkle the saffron threads, if using, into 1 cup of the stock and let dissolve.
- Into a medium sauté pan, drizzle a glug of olive oil and add 1 of the garlic cloves and half of the diced onion. Simmer over a low to medium heat until soft, about 5 minutes. Add the tomatoes, basil, and a large pinch of salt. Cook down until the tomatoes have softened and the mixture begins to gel, about 10 minutes.
- In a large, deep frying pan or a pot, pour in a glug of olive oil and sauté the rest of the onion and garlic over medium-low heat until softened and translucent. If using the pepperoncini, they can be sautéed now as well.
- Add the white wine to the pan and raise the heat to allow the alcohol to evaporate.
- Reduce the heat to medium and add the fresh tomato sauce as well as the stock, including the saffron-infused stock. Add salt and pepper to taste. Let cook for a few minutes.
- The sauce should now be at a slow boil. Add the clams and mussels that are still in their shells and cover. After 2 minutes, add the shrimp and cover. After 2 more minutes, add the fish and the reserved clam and mussel meat. Cover and cook for about 2 minutes. Turn off the heat and add a drizzle of extra-virgin olive oil. Taste and add more salt or pepper if needed. Cover with the lid slightly askew and let rest for about 10 minutes.
- Ladle into large bowls, sprinkling each with chopped parsley and a drizzle of olive oil. Serve with the toasted bread.

— SPAGHETTI CON ZUCCHINE ALLA NERANO —

About ½ quart sunflower oil or vegetable oil, or, if you choose, olive oil

8 to 10 small zucchine

1 ½ cups chopped fresh basil

Sea salt to taste

Extra-virgin olive oil

1 pound spaghetti

3 cups grated Parmigiano-Reggiano

- Put the sunflower oil in a large pot and bring to a low boil over medium-high heat.
- Slice the zucchini into thin rounds and fry in the oil until it is golden brown. Remove and set aside on paper towels.
- Sprinkle with the basil and the salt to taste.
- Transfer to a bowl and drizzle liberally with olive oil.
- Boil the pasta until al dente and strain, reserving about 2 cups of the pasta water.
- Place the cooked pasta in a large pan or pot over low heat along with the zucchine mixture and combine gently. Add the pasta water, a little at a time, to create a creamy texture. You may not use all of the pasta water. Now add some of the Parmigiano to the mixture and continue to combine by stirring gently and tossing. When the mixture has a slight creaminess, remove from the stove and serve immediately.

Note: The zucchine mixture can be refrigerated for about 5 days for use at a later date. Best to bring it to room temperature before using.

— PASTA ALLA NORMA —

2 large garlic cloves, halved

Extra-virgin olive oil

2 large eggplants, diced

Kosher salt

5 cups marinara sauce

1 pound pasta (rigatoni, ziti, or a thick spaghetti)

A handful of basil, roughly chopped

A handful of grated ricotta salata or Pecorino

- In a very large frying pan, fry the garlic in a glug of oil over low heat for about 2 minutes. Add the eggplants, raise the heat to medium, and cook for about 15 minutes, until slightly golden. Salt to taste.
- Add the marinara sauce and cook for about 5 minutes more.
- Cook the pasta and drain, reserving ½ cup of the water.
- Stir the reserved pasta water into the pan mixture and sprinkle with the basil. Measure 4 cups of the sauce and put it in a serving bowl. Add the drained pasta to the pan with the remainder of the sauce and gently stir it all together. Sprinkle with grated ricotta salata or Pecorino and serve with the extra sauce on the side.

— SIMPLE CHICKEN STOCK —

1 chicken carcass (without meat) and 1 whole chicken without breast meat (or 2 of either one)

10 mixed peppercorns

1 medium yellow onion, skin on, cut in half

1 medium red onion, skin on, cut in half

2 garlic cloves, skin on

2 celery stalks, quartered

2 carrots, quartered

A handful of parsley

2 bay leaves

Salt

1 sprig rosemary

2 sprigs thyme

- If you are using a whole chicken, cut it in pieces at the leg joints. Put the carcass and chicken pieces into a stockpot and cover with water. Bring to a boil and skim off the scum that rises to the top. Add the other ingredients and simmer, partially covered, for as long as you want but at least 2 hours.
- Strain through a sieve into some vessel and allow to cool, then refrigerate, or divide among freezer bags and freeze.

— LAMB CHOPS —

INGREDIENTS

A glug of extra-virgin olive oil

3 garlic cloves, halved

10 to 12 lamb chops, salted an hour before using

White wine

1 teaspoon fresh rosemary leaves

1 teaspoon fresh thyme leaves

- In a large cast-iron pan, splash in a tiny bit of the oil and add the garlic. Cook over low heat for about 3 minutes. Remove and set aside. Raise the heat to medium-high and sear the lamb chops until they are browned, 2 to 3 minutes on each side. You may do this in two batches.
- Remove the chops from the pan and set them aside on a platter. Add a splash of white wine to the pan, and perhaps a little water, and deglaze. Return the garlic to the pan along with the herbs. Cook for maybe a minute. Pour over the lamb chops and tent with foil for 5 minutes before serving.

— PASTA FAGIOLI (MY WAY) —

Extra-virgin olive oil

1 medium onion, sliced

2 garlic cloves, halved

½ bunch cavolo nero, roughly chopped

Three 14-ounce cans cannellini beans

3 cups Chicken Stock (page 253) or vegetable stock

2 to 3 cups marinara sauce

1 pound small pasta, like ditali or gnocchetti sardi

Salt

Freshly ground black pepper

Parmigiano-Reggiano or Pecorino, for serving (optional)

- Pour a glug of the oil into a medium pot and sauté the onion and garlic over medium-low heat until soft. At the same time, boil the cavolo nero in a small pot of salted water.
- Add the beans, stock, and marinara to the pan with the onion and garlic and stir together. Cook over low heat.
- When the cavolo nero is soft, strain it, add it to the bean mixture, and stir. Continue to cook on a low simmer with the lid askew for about 15 minutes.
- In the meantime, boil the pasta in salted water according to the directions on the package. When it's done, strain it, reserving about a cup of the water, and place it in a large bowl. Add about 2 cups of the bean mixture to the pasta along with some of the pasta water and a drizzle of oil and mix.

- Salt to taste and divide among 4 bowls. Add more bean mixture to each bowl along with a drizzle of oil. Sprinkle with pepper and Parmigiano or Pecorino, if using.
- Variation: Loosely scramble 2 large eggs in a pan with olive oil. Then add one portion of the finished recipe above, including the pasta, and toss together. Finish with grated Parmigiano or Pecorino and a drizzle of olive oil.

Printed in Dunstable, United Kingdom